2021

- Commanding Life -

365 Days of Inspiration and Affirmations

2021 Commanding Life 365 Days of
Inspiration and Affirmations

Copyright © 2021 by Commanding Life

All rights reserved.

No part of this book may be reproduced, stored in a retrieval system, or transmitted in any form or by any means, electronic, mechanical, recording, photocopying, scanning, or otherwise, without written permission from the author.

For information about permission to reproduce selections from this book, e-mail hello@commandinglife.com

Cover photo by Human via Unsplash

www.CommandingLife.com

ISBN 978-1-7325400-5-7

What I welcome into my life for 2021

January 1, 2021

This January, I am receiving more. I am trusting that I am being offered more chances to create and elevate to the life I want. I am thriving and living with more love, happiness, and peace. I am welcoming more abundance. I am being blessed with more opportunities, and more doors are opening for me. I am releasing the past, and I am moving forward with faith that more miracles will manifest for me.

AFFIRM

I am ready to receive more blessings.

January 2, 2021

If you are praying for prosperity, try planting and preparing for a harvest. If you are praying for the hurt to go away, practice healing with self-care. If you are praying for true love, start with self-compassion. If you are praying with impatience, focus on gratitude for your blessings. Whatever you are praying for, create it in your life, and more will manifest. Prayers are answered on the journey, not at the destination.

AFFIRM

I am in a season of abundance.

January 3, 2021

Don't get mad at someone for crossing the line, set boundaries. Don't feel defeated because you aren't where you want to be; focus on what needs to get done to thrive. Don't get sad it didn't work out, find the lesson, and level up to more. Whatever you think is blocking you is Divinely sent to create the ultimate you. You are destined for a life vision more significant than you can perceive. Keep going.

AFFIRM

I am destined for great things.

January 4, 2021

When you truly recognize your worth, you transform your life beyond self-imposed limitations that leave you in lack. Understanding you deserve all allows you to believe in more, welcome more, and go after more. Start with defining how valuable you are, then set expectations for your life, and welcome others to meet you there. In believing you are priceless, the unlimited possibilities for your life will manifest.

AFFIRM

I am aware of my full worth.

January 5, 2021

You don't have to be perfect to be lovable. You don't have to be fully healed to pursue wholeness. You don't have to have anything to welcome abundance. You don't have to be passive to live in peace. You don't have to be lacking before you figure out you deserve more. You don't need to overcome fear; you just have to choose faith. Whatever you want does not have a precondition; want it, then go for it.

AFFIRM

I am whole and worthy of all I desire.

January 6, 2021

When you choose to heal, you begin the process of advocating for yourself. Healing is about leaving the effects of the past behind you to focus on what needs to be done in the now to be your best. Start with pursuing what makes you happy and fulfilled. Practicing positive emotions like gratitude will support your journey to joy. You feel blessed when you acknowledge you are. Today make wellbeing your priority.

AFFIRM

I am pursuing what makes me happy.

January 7, 2021

There will be times you want to give up; rest but never quit on your happiness. There will be times you feel impatient waiting for your work to pay off; stay motivated by being grateful for your progress. There will be times you are fearful; choose faith and trust your miracles will manifest. Every experience prepares you to weather the next. It will all be worth it once you step into the sunshine.

AFFIRM

I am ready to step into the sunshine.

January 8, 2021

Miracles are manifesting in your life; don't be distracted by the deficiencies. You have made progress without knowing where you were going, and you took chances without the surety of winning. Keep going and focus on the promise of prosperity, not the pace. Big things can happen in short periods; get ready to be amazed at the abundance on its way to you.

AFFIRM

I am a magnet for abundance.

January 9, 2021

People chase what they think is best without consideration for what they need to be happy. They build their life on momentary wants, not on what motivates them to keep going in any situation. You are repeatedly tested not because you are a failure; but because you are not aligned with your truest needs. When you find who you are, your deepest desires are revealed. Move from surviving to thriving. Freedom comes when you focus on your core desires.

AFFIRM

I am welcoming my thriving.

January 10, 2021

Find your happiness by focusing on how you want to feel. It might be what you need to reveal your way forward. Concentrating on your joy is not selfish; it is self-first. Start with exploring what fills you up and energizes you. 'You' time will help you to prepare for catering to others. Despite what you face, figure out what you need to thrive, and you will triumph.

AFFIRM

I am mastering what I need to pursue my win.

January 11, 2021

Get comfortable with the word 'wait.' Trust that a delay is never a denial of what you desire. Sometimes, you are slowed down to learn your true worth. Life is trying to show you the area you have prepared for your blessings may not be big enough. Don't get fearful; get faithful, and focus on what needs to be done before you get your 'yes.' Don't let 'hold' make you feel helpless; get hopeful for a bigger harvest.

AFFIRM

I am hopeful I will be abundant.

January 12, 2021

Say goodbye to what wants to go; release it with grace. Say hello to the blessings coming; welcome them with gratitude. Focus on what is present; trust more will come. When you think you were neglected, the Universe will show you it was silently preparing more than you can imagine. Don't lose hope because you cannot see a way, rejoice and expect your miracle. You are always given what you need to thrive.

AFFIRM

I am always given what I need to thrive.

January 13, 2021

No one is coming to save you or bring you happiness. You have to do that for yourself. What keeps you from thriving is the self-imposed limits you created from your pain. Choose to see the infinite possibilities of your potential. Reclaim your worth and acknowledge you are capable of being all you desire. Love, abundance, and success are already within you, waiting to be unleashed. Confidently be yourself; you are amazing.

AFFIRM

I am confident in my abilities, and I am amazing.

January 14, 2021

Sometimes you need to fall before you rise, fail before you succeed, lose before you gain, and pause before you can move forward. Credit yourself for the strength you found when you were unexpectedly pushed from your comfort zone, yet you still kept going. Continue to care about how you feel as you deliberately speak kind, uplifting words to yourself. Focus on the life you want to create and keep elevating. You are deserving of all.

AFFIRM

I am deserving of all that I desire.

January 15, 2021

Sometimes, the process of healing can hurt more than what caused the pain. Facing yourself can be scary, but it is necessary if you want to regain your happiness. Choices made from unresolved hurt can create a massive mess with your future decisions. Focus on your positives and potential; they will help you push past your pain to start from a place of love, not hurt. Changed behavior can add to the power of your prayers.

AFFIRM

I am improving daily.

January 16, 2021

Instead of overthinking, maintain your peace by finding balance in doing what you enjoy. Instead of battling your fears, maintain your faith, and trust all is well. Instead of focusing on lack, maintain gratitude for what you do have. Instead of concentrating on loneliness, maintain the loving relationships that surround you. Fighting negative feelings can consume your happiness; maintaining your positive emotions require less energy.

AFFIRM

I am finding balance and harmony in my life.

January 17, 2021

When you ask for something, you have to be willing to receive it; no matter if it does not unfold the way you think. You will be put in situations to grow up, glow up, or get out. You will grow up when you learn the lesson. You will glow up when you understand your true worth. You will get out when you release what is keeping you small. The ease of this transition depends on your resistance to the process of change. The Universe is always trying to level you up.

AFFIRM

I am leveling up to more.

January 18, 2021

You don't need someone to change before you find peace. You don't need to be successful before you feel abundant. You don't need the love of another before you begin to love yourself. Yes, it is easier to blame everything else but yourself, but your happiness is your responsibility. The moment you understand you are 'response able,' you begin to take charge of how you feel and the choices you make.

AFFIRM

I am response-ABLE.

January 19, 2021

Understand you cannot control the actions of others, but you can manage your response to them. Never allow anyone to pull you back to their level when you have put in the effort to elevate to where you are. You have done the work to become a better version of yourself, set your boundaries, and define how others relate to you. Don't get distracted by things that have nothing to do with your goals. Self-first is not selfish.

AFFIRM

I am self-first and self-compassionate.

January 20, 2021

Your strength is built from every brick thrown at you. Your abundance is cultivated from every seed you have ever planted. Your peace is gained from every moment you sit still and embrace your faith. Your clarity is created in every moment you focus on your happiness. You can't wish for more and not put in any effort to make it. Be patient with the process that produces what you want. A strong foundation is not built by chance but by choice.

AFFIRM

I am patient with the process.

January 21, 2021

Don't be afraid of words like failure, stressed, overwhelmed, depressed, or fatigued. They are natural states that you must go through to get to the breakthrough. They teach you what you don't want and empower you to go after what you do what. Everyone deals with struggle differently; some people move through their phases faster than others. Never be ashamed of the pace you push through. In every moment, you are doing the best you can.

AFFIRM

I am doing the best I can.

January 22, 2021

When you asked, and the answer was, "Stop, not yet, or wait," smile. The pause is the Universe responding with, "I have something better for you." Requests are never denied; they are delayed when you haven't asked for big enough. Instead of getting frustrated about being blocked, take a moment to rejoice in the better being sent to you. Don't get stuck on the stop; get excited about the possibilities.

AFFIRM

I am excited about my possibilities.

January 23, 2021

Take a moment to acknowledge the positive transformations that can come from slowing down. You can learn to listen more attentively to what your soul wants. You can use compassion to repair and restore important relationships. You can create more clarity with what you want for your life. Sometimes the ability to rest gets you ready for when you get your go.

AFFIRM

I am getting ready for my win.

January 24, 2021

When you remove what holds you back from what you want, what you need will show up. The problem isn't your desires; it is the limiting beliefs about what you deserve. A scarcity mindset blocks abundance. Reliving the hurt keeps you from allowing wholeness into your life. The need for validation traps you in someone else's idea of who you are. Work on releasing the limits and welcome the win.

AFFIRM

I am releasing my limits and welcoming my win.

January 25, 2021

Yes, you are adjusting to the current circumstances, but don't forget to create the improvements you want to see. We all deal with change differently; remember to keep encouraging yourself to live the best you can by focusing on your happiness. Start each day with gratitude; it will boost your outlook. Mindfully living can improve your capability and develop your COPE-ability.

AFFIRM

I am capable and cope-able.

January 26, 2021

Healing begins when you care about how you feel. When you give in to negative emotions like shame, unworthiness, or guilt, you challenge your wellbeing. Don't let circumstances make you lose sight of who you are; remember your capabilities. You, like everyone else, deserve to achieve whatever you want. There will always be something that will test you; never let it distract you from who you are meant to be.

AFFIRM

I am deserving of success.

January 27, 2021

Forgive yourself for the times you stayed stuck in the past before you accepted the present. Forgive yourself for feeling like a victim before you found your victory. Forgive yourself for the journey you took to understand what you deserve. Forgive yourself for the pace it takes you to learn your purpose. Forgive yourself as many times as you need to develop the self-compassion it takes for you to keep going.

AFFIRM

I am forgiving myself and focusing forward.

January 28, 2021

When you doubt whether you deserve happiness or not, remember the improvements you made. The mindset you changed. The abundance you created from nothing. The mountains you conquered. The stormy seas you navigated through. The wins you fought for, and the progress you pushed through despite the struggle. Don't stop now; keep going. You did that; you deserve the best life has to offer.

AFFIRM

I am welcoming the best life has to offer.

January 29, 2021

When you are struggling, believing you can get through it might seem impossible, but don't let the thought of creating change defeat you before you take action. The hardest part of any struggle is learning to think and feel differently while trying to stay hopeful. Yes, the first step toward change will be your toughest, but it will be the most rewarding. Go for your happiness; you have what it takes to progress.

AFFIRM

I am going for my happiness.

January 30, 2021

Today is a great day to count your blessings from the past month. Take a moment to stop, look, and love. Stop and feel gratitude for what you overcame to get to where you are. Look and observe how beautifully your progress has unfolded. Love and accept who you are becoming. You are doing the best you can; appreciate and celebrate every step you make forward.

AFFIRM

I am appreciating and celebrating every step I take forward.

January 31, 2021

The Universe always has three answers: "yes," "not right now," or "I have better for you." "Yes," happens when you are ready, and the timing is right. "Not right now," is reassurance you need to get ready for more. "I have better for you," indicates you are worthy of receiving more than you can imagine. Trust that the answer you get is for your good. You are never given a promise without the right provision, path, or opportunity to prepare.

AFFIRM

I am on the right path for my success.

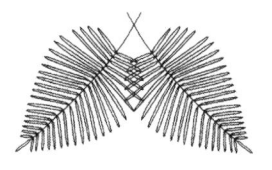

February 1, 2021

This February, I am focused on who I AM. I am loving, and I am loved. I am appreciative, and I am appreciated. I am blessed, and I am a blessing. I am happy, and I am happily creating more. I am supported, and I am supportive. I am at peace, and I am living in peace. Thank you, Universe, for helping me be the best that I am destined to be.

AFFIRM

I am joyously working on who I need to be.

February 2, 2021

Release yourself from your past burdens by letting things go and allowing people and situations to be. Stop looking for explanations, apologies, closure, validation, or answers that might never come. Move past living a life centered on what others did or did not do and focus on how you want to feel in the now. Peace comes when you realize your choices create your happiness. Your life is your responsibility.

AFFIRM

I am making great choices for my happiness.

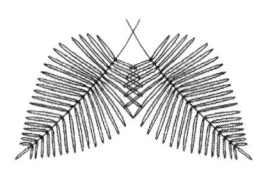

February 3, 2021

Work on who you are; it will get you where you want to go. Life never blocks your blessings; it only sends challenges to prepare you to receive more. Your miracles are already arranged; they are waiting for you to get ready to collect. Do the self-work needed to manifest what you want; it will be worth it. You must work on your wholeness and healing to master handling the abundant blessings coming your way.

AFFIRM

I am working on my wholeness.

February 4, 2021

You weren't abandoned; you were left alone to learn how to love yourself. You weren't hurt; you were being shown how to heal what you don't face. You weren't rejected; you were being redirected to better. You weren't delayed; you were being slowed down to discover what you deserve. You weren't punished; you were being pushed to more. You are never losing, only learning and leveling up.

AFFIRM

I am learning and leveling up.

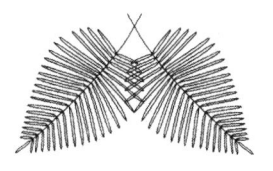

February 5, 2021

Let today's mood be praising, thanking, rejoicing, and celebrating. Praising for all the spontaneous blessings showing up for you. Thanking for the abundance flowing smoothly to you. Rejoicing for what you have overcome to get to your place of peace. Celebrating for everything working out for you. Your mood can manifest your miracles.

AFFIRM

I am manifesting miracles.

February 6, 2021

At this moment, you are blessed with everything you need to move forward. Release the limiting thoughts of lack and fear. More is already on the way to you. Trust you are never given a seed to plant without the provisions needed to grow into the life you want. Don't delay the manifestation with doubt in what you deserve. Remember, keep the faith; big things can happen in short periods.

AFFIRM

I am blessed with what I need to move forward.

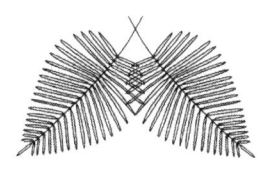

February 7, 2021

The true love you wish for is being prepared for you. The big break you are asking for is aligning bigger than you can imagine. The prosperity you are patiently waiting for is being packaged and positioned. Remember, the miracle you are expecting can manifest at any instant. The minute you trust that what you are praying for is a done deal, it's the moment it gets delivered.

AFFIRM

I am trusting that what I pray for is a done deal.

February 8, 2021

Never let what you don't have, distract you from what has manifested. Take a moment to acknowledge what you have accomplished and celebrate the work you have done to change and push forward. Praise how far you have courageously traveled to move away from the hurt. You have a lot around you to fill you with gratitude. Slow down and appreciate your progress. You did that.

AFFIRM

I am grateful for my progress.

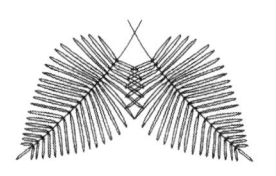

February 9, 2021

Surrendering to the process is not about giving up on your dreams; it is letting go of how you think they should materialize. Release how you believe it must unfold and focus on the 'why' you want your desires to manifest. Everything you want is because you think you will be happy when you get it. Try a new approach, focus on being joyful on the way to what you want, and your desires will materialize faster.

AFFIRM

I am joyful on my journey.

February 10, 2021

Release your grip on the little and allow the more to manifest. Release the need to control how it should go and tune in for the inspired action to get it done. Release the limiting beliefs about what you think you deserve and allow bigger blessings to be created. Release the hurt of the past, and welcome the healing trying to get through the walls you built. Sometimes you have to release before you can receive.

AFFIRM

I am releasing and making room to receive.

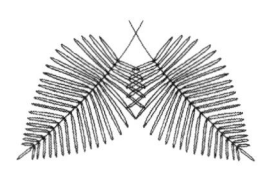

February 11, 2021

You should never have to demonstrate your worth to anyone; stop trying. Prove it to yourself by believing you have enough, and you give enough. Your value does not diminish because of your experiences; it is revealed. Trust something good is always happening for you, even when you cannot see it. When you believe you are worthy of all, you will begin to receive all. My friend, you are already enough.

AFFIRM

I am already enough.

February 12, 2021

Impatience can be doubt in what you believe you deserve. When you are rushing results, you miss out on the reason for the delay. What if you are being made to wait because what you asked for wasn't big enough? Don't waste the in-between time worrying; use it to request more. Trust everything you want, plus more will manifest. The wait means you aren't done defining the fullness of your desires.

AFFIRM

I am aligning with what I desire.

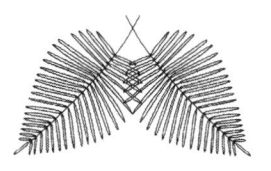

February 13, 2021

Every phase of your life is designed to teach you how to level up to more. You are meant to shape your life from your experiences, not carry the hurt into the next chapters. Be cautious because hurt people can hurt people and themselves. In releasing the pain from the past, you develop the skills to create what you want in your future. You are a creator, not a carrier.

AFFIRM

I am a creator, not a carrier.

February 14, 2021

When you choose to heal, you begin to advocate for yourself by understanding what you truly deserve. Healing is about leaving the effects of the past behind to focus on what needs to be done right now to feel your best. The daily practice of positive emotions like gratitude can support your journey to joy. You feel blessed when you acknowledge you are. Make wellbeing your primary priority.

AFFIRM

I am making my wellbeing a priority.

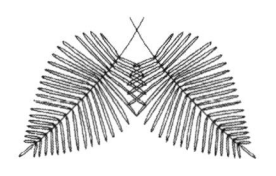

February 15, 2021

You can choose to look forward or backward from where you are standing, but you cannot do both. When people look back, they typically focus on what went wrong. When you decide to look forward, you unleash your power of creating what you can make right. Choose one direction and concentrate on it. You are capable of having everything you want. Happy people focus forward.

AFFIRM

I am focused forward.

February 16, 2021

Overthinking can originate from self-doubt, past outcomes, and experiences. Survival mode prevents you from seeing you are already thriving. When your thought process is focused on what can go wrong, it blocks your ability to find solutions. Trust you already have what you need to find a way out. You are capable enough and creative enough to succeed. You've got this. Keep going.

AFFIRM

I am capable and creative enough to succeed.

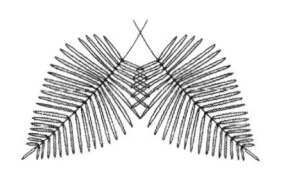

February 17, 2021

Unlock your full potential by concentrating on your possibilities rather than your pain. Everyone has a past where someone has wronged them, or something did not go according to plan. Staying there locks you into victim mode and keeps you away from happiness. Switch to victor mode by accepting you are more than your past and worthy of a great future. You are a powerful creator; start creating.

AFFIRM

I am a powerful creator.

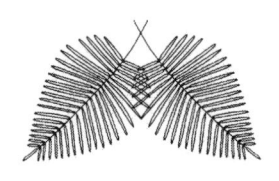

February 18, 2021

When a challenge occurs, don't get discouraged; stay focused. Delays only mean you are in the process of clarifying and fine-tuning your desires. Life is about sifting through and sorting out who you are and what you want. Trials help you define what happiness and fulfillment really mean to you. You must first have a problem to solve before you have the enjoyment of the solution. The unfolding is where miracles happen.

AFFIRM

I am finding solutions all around me.

February 19, 2021

Many people devote their lives to changing what's going on around them, and they fail to see the power to create what they want comes from within. The abundance you want starts with worth. The love you desire begins with understanding what you deserve. The peace you pursue originates from being present. When you take the time to adjust your inner dial to thriving, you fine-tune your happiness and prosperity.

AFFIRM

I am fine-tuning my happiness and pursuing my prosperity.

February 20, 2021

How you respond to a situation is about you, it is not about the other person. Yes, people can be mean and do hurtful things, but you have the power of choice in your reaction. You can allow them to pull you down to their level, or you can stay vibrating higher and focusing forward. How you respond determines your happiness, not theirs.

AFFIRM

I am vibrating higher and focusing forward.

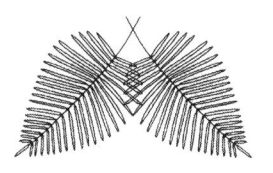

February 21, 2021

You cannot let the right experiences in if you don't move past the bad ones. Yes, you have been wounded, but it won't fully heal if you keep picking at the scar. It is natural to want to protect your heart, but you must find a way to let the past go and allow the good to happen for you. Be mindful, the barriers you built to protect can also block what you want to manifest.

AFFIRM

I am leaving the past where it belongs, behind me.

February 22, 2021

Cycles of resilience, rejection, receiving, and redemption are all important to any journey. Resilience is where you learn your strength to bend without breaking. Rejection is where you are taught to reclaim your true worth. Receiving is where you use gratitude to focus on your blessings. Redemption is where you celebrate your triumphs. Whatever stage you are in, know you have what it takes to get through them all. Keep going.

AFFIRM

I am celebrating my wins.

February 23, 2021

Some people are afraid, not because they fear the mountain, but because they do not trust they have what it takes to make it to the top. Remember, everyone is given what they need to succeed. Right now, you have enough to create more. Yes, you have stumbled, but you were supported and never fell off. Take a moment today to count your blessings and celebrate your progress.

AFFIRM

I am counting my blessings and praising my progress.

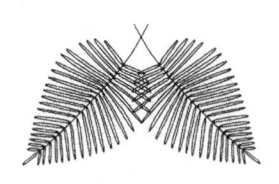

February 24, 2021

Bad experiences shouldn't stop you from building a better future. You must have the courage to focus on how you want to feel now to fuel what you can create tomorrow. Your feelings determine your focus. If you concentrate on the positive, you find positive. Stop complaining about what you are going through and start 'thanking' for your blessings. Every closed door is redirecting you to rewarding opportunities.

AFFIRM

I am thankful for my blessings.

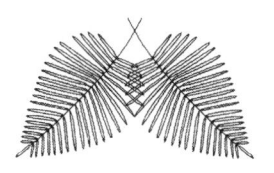

February 25, 2021

Don't let doubt keep you from doing. Combat the feeling by choosing to have faith over fear. Fear keeps you stuck, and faith keeps you focused forward. Instead, concentrate on what is working in your favor. Use your gratitude to change any moment into one filled with grace. If you believe in the blessings coming, you won't stress about what is happening. Trust things are working out for you.

AFFIRM

I am trusting things are working in my favor.

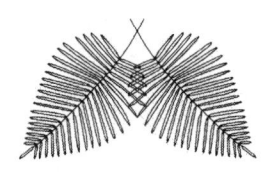

February 26, 2021

Always believe that everything is working out for you. When you think that things are falling apart, understand it is only falling into place. Sometimes foundations need to break for you to rebuild and become. Life will upgrade and transform you for your promise. Remember, the more you put into your path, the higher the levels and blessings attained.

AFFIRM

I am leveling up to my promise.

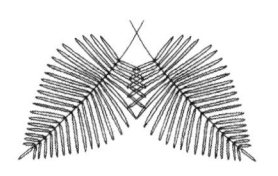

February 27, 2021

Remember, in every situation, you have control over whether you react or respond. Survival is when you react to your circumstances without much consideration for your actions. Reacting gives the situation control over you. Thriving is when you respond to your situation with carefully thought out actions. This response puts you in control of what you create. You have the power to choose how you win.

AFFIRM

I am in control of what I create.

February 28, 2021

When you haven't forgiven someone, it means you still want something from them. What if the explanation or apology never came? Then it is up to you to release yourself from being trapped in the past. Forgive, move forward, and stop wishing it was different. Yes, you were hurt, but it is your responsibility to heal. No one owes you anything. You, however, owe yourself everything, especially happiness.

AFFIRM

I am forgiving and moving forward.

March 1, 2021

This March, I am centering myself with Divine grace and gratitude for my blessings. I am faith-full that everything is working out for me. As I release the thoughts that do not serve my happiness, I welcome the pouring of prosperity and wellbeing into my life. My heart and soul are at peace because I trust life is for me. Thank you, Source, for protecting, supporting, providing for, and loving me always.

AFFIRM

I am welcoming my wellbeing.

March 2, 2021

Self-love is the feeling, and self-care is the action. You can have self-love but fall short in your self-care practice. You must put yourself first so that you can then be the best for others. "Self-first" is not selfish when you take the time to create habits that support how you feel and the thriving you want in your life. When you align your positive intentions with inspired actions, your happiness will blossom.

AFFIRM

I am taking inspired action.

March 3, 2021

You cannot worry about lack and expect to receive blessings. You cannot doubt your abilities and plan to create all that you want. You cannot fear the future and stay stuck in the past. You cannot close off your heart and expect love to get in. Make a change by accepting where you are and start there to produce the life you want. Use what you are given to create your desires. Trust the Universe will always meet your needs.

AFFIRM

I am using what I am given to create my desires.

March 4, 2021

If you're feeling impatient today, ground yourself with gratitude. Gratitude for how far you have traveled emotionally, spiritually, and mentally. Gratitude for the strength it took to overcome and triumph at this moment. Gratitude that you are miraculously being protected and provided for. Gratitude that you have what it takes to keep going and winning. You are blessed.

AFFIRM

I am being protected and provided for.

March 5, 2021

Having faith in your possibilities does not mean you will have it easy; it is about finding comfort in knowing you will eventually succeed despite setbacks. Keep putting up a good fight to stay in the race, and don't quit because you feel challenged. No one is exempt from trying times. Trust what you diligently work for will materialize soon. Use the power of faith to keep climbing even when you cannot see the top.

AFFIRM

I am using my faith to keep climbing to the top.

March 6, 2021

The Universe conspires in your favor when you commit to your happiness. The infinite possibilities of what you can create are based on your actions, your relationship with yourself, and the attention you place on your emotional wealth. Your heart is the seed of your life; what you hold in it will be what matures. Yes, miracles manifest from dirt, but the seed must be lovingly nurtured and healthy to thrive. Better cannot grow from bitter.

AFFIRM

I am focused on being better.

March 7, 2021

Appreciate the lessons learned from your experiences. Without them, you would not have been able to move forward. Like a video game, every victory unlocks what you need to level up faster. Focus on what you need to master at this moment to create the life you want. It is not about where you are; it is about discovering and embracing who you need to be to get to where you are going. You've got this.

AFFIRM

I am creating the life I want.

March 8, 2021

Experiences can take, push, or pull, and that can be draining to your energy. However, focusing on positive emotions can activate your ability to move forward. Use your gratitude to help you stay grounded and focused on your victory. Don't forget to pour into your self-love reserves so you can draw on them when needed. You have to be good before you can be of good. Self-first is not selfish.

AFFIRM

I am grounded in gratitude.

March 9, 2021

When you don't like your reality, it is challenging to find things to appreciate in your life. However, it is important to make peace with where you are while working on where you want to go. It's not about settling for your life; it's about finding solutions through a positive attitude. You are always moving forward; focus on the progress and release the control of the pace. Big possibilities cannot be created from limited thinking.

AFFIRM

I am releasing my focus on the pace.

March 10, 2021

You cannot expect someone to love you right when you haven't committed to your wellbeing. It is your responsibility to clear the confusion surrounding how you give and receive love. The best way to improve your beliefs about love is through a consistent practice of self-care and self-compassion. Don't let a poorly executed chapter taint your entire love story. Real love requires patience and work. You deserve the love you give.

AFFIRM

I am deserving of the love I give.

March 11, 2021

No one is ever ready for the tests they face, yet they still forge forward. No one is ever prepared to carry burdens, but they build strength along the way. No one's life is perfect, but they develop the grace needed to win. Life is about doing your best on the ride, not the arrival. Make the most of your journey by developing your discernment, practicing patience, and acknowledging you are always being blessed and guided along the way.

AFFIRM

I am making the most of my journey.

March 12, 2021

Stay patient and faithful. Believe your blessings are being built and held until you are ready. Every experience is designed to prepare you to collect. Trust you are moving closer to your more every day. Hearts must be opened to receive, shoulders strengthened to carry, and mindsets mastered for you to maintain abundance. Today make room for your delivery. Big beautiful blessings can manifest in short timeframes.

AFFIRM

I am patient and faithful.

March 13, 2021

When you ignore the nudges to step up, life will push you to level up. This can feel terrifying because everything appears as if it is falling out from under you. To secure your foundation, you will need to let go of what's not supporting you. Life is only trying to show you that where you are is not the furthest you can reach. Rise to your better. Don't let comfort on the lower ground prevent you from stepping into your highest potential.

AFFIRM

I am stepping into my highest potential.

March 14, 2021

Today refuse to let the doubt within you win. Fight the feeling by believing in your capabilities. Use the affirmation: "I am choosing to have faith." Repeat it as many times as you need and conquer the doubt with DO. Do believe you are worthy. Do believe you have the power to overcome. Most of all, do believe you can create the life you want. Your life will transform when you change your doubt into do.

AFFIRM

I am making changes and transforming my life.

March 15, 2021

Honor how you feel at this moment. From time to time, we all get tired, overwhelmed, and feel uncertain. If you are weary, rest, and recoup. If you are stuck, sit, listen, and regain your footing before you move forward. If you are overwhelmed, take a deep breath and slow down to figure it out. Don't judge yourself for needing a break. Be kind to yourself and remember you are always doing the best you can.

AFFIRM

I am doing the best I can.

March 16, 2021

Paths are not cleared until you come to them. Doors aren't opened until you knock, and obstacles aren't removed until you reach them. Don't worry about what you think might happen; focus on what is happening and do your best. You have always been provided for one way or the other. Trust that you will get the Divine support you need and keep going.

AFFIRM

I am Divinely supported.

March 17, 2021

Don't make decisions based on exhausting emotions like fear and doubt; all they do is distract and drain you into feeling incapable. These emotions send you the wrong signal about your ability to create a way out, don't trust them. Today if you feel tired, relax. Use this moment to restore, rebuild, and regain your strength. Know the difference between resting and giving up.

AFFIRM

I am not giving up on my happiness.

March 18, 2021

You are always attracting the support and resources needed to complete your vision. Trust the Universe is working behind the scenes to move you in the direction of your dreams. Use the delays to master your commitment and determination to succeed. Don't give up; keep going. You have what it takes. You're not far from what you desire. It will happen soon. Trust the process.

AFFIRM

I am trusting the process.

March 19, 2021

Self-confidence is developed with each decision made. Trust things are always working out for your good. When your choices have the desired outcome, you generate trust in your abilities; that's winning. When your choices have unwanted results, you learn who you are; that's wisdom. Both help you grow and master how to get life right. Every decision cultivates your discernment and helps you level up.

AFFIRM

I am trusting in my abilities, and I am leveling up.

March 20, 2021

You cannot lead yourself to success when you feel like a victim. You become the victor when you take responsibility for where you are and commit to where you want to go. Start with prioritizing how you want to feel and use it to create what is important to you. When you make happiness your primary focus, nothing will prevent you from crossing the finish line. Keep going; you are stronger than you think.

AFFIRM

I am strong, and I am a victor.

March 21, 2021

Forgive yourself for the times you stayed stuck in the past. Credit yourself for the courage it took to move forward and believe you can create your future. Forgive yourself for feeling like you lost. Credit yourself for getting back in the race to pursue your victory. Develop the self-compassion that is needed to forgive as many times as necessary. Never be afraid to start again. You deserve all.

AFFIRM

I am deserving of all.

March 22, 2021

Don't lose faith right before the fruition; focus on what needs to get done for the miracle to manifest. Sometimes your dreams are too small for the larger vision that needs time to unfold. Use the time to understand the magnitude of your worth. Find pleasure in being patient. A delay is never a denial of desires. Don't let the wait make you feel helpless; get hopeful for the biggest blessing you can imagine.

AFFIRM

I am hopeful for big blessings.

March 23, 2021

At this instant, you have so much to be thankful for. You are surrounded by people who love you despite how you feel about where you are. You are triumphing over battles no one knew you were fighting. You are healing from the hurt that held you back from going after your ALL. You are shedding the old and creating new blessings. You are manifesting miracles in every moment. Celebrate you.

AFFIRM

I am celebrating who I am.

March 24, 2021

Facing past trauma can be scary. However, it is necessary if you want to be happy and move forward. Yes, healing can take longer than what caused the pain, but choices made from the filters of unresolved hurt can keep you stuck. Focus on your positive attributes and your unlimited potential. They will help you push past your pain to create beauty from a place of love. You owe it to yourself to heal.

AFFIRM

I am focused on the good within me.

March 25, 2021

Keep elevating by telling yourself positive statements about your progress. Release the need for external validation; it only distracts you from how empowered you feel because of your commitment to your happiness. Focus on why you want the win, not the recognition from others. Remember, you are moving forward and doing the best you can with what you know at every moment. Give yourself credit for how much you have evolved.

AFFIRM

I am giving myself credit for my progress.

March 26, 2021

For some, their happiness is a choice between fight or flight. Only you can decide if you believe in the possibility of your dreams or doubt your ability to have what you want. Faith is your fight. Fear is your flight. Before you give up, appreciate that you are given another chance to create what you want every morning. Don't let doubt deter you from actively creating your vision. Only you can fight for your future.

AFFIRM

I am focused on my fruitful future.

March 27, 2021

You can control whether you react or respond. Reacting to your circumstances without consideration for your actions gives the situation control over you. Responding to your situation with carefully thought out actions puts you in control of what you create. You have the power to choose how you win and make things work out for you. Stop reacting. Start responding.

AFFIRM

I am in control of what I can create.

March 28, 2021

Miracles always manifest when you aren't looking. When you release the focus on when and how your blessings will arrive, only then will they show up and surprise you. Giving up control requires concentration. The work is in the wait. Master your focus on what you are doing now and how it contributes to where you are going. Being present is the best present you can give your future self.

AFFIRM

I am living in the moment.

March 29, 2021

You must know pain to know love. Know struggle to recognize success. Be at the bottom to understand the importance of the rise to the top. Be thankful for it all, and keep growing and going. Use hope and faith to strengthen you for the journey. Hope that nothing remains the same, and confidence that you are destined for the best. Climb, my friend, climb.

AFFIRM

I am destined to reach the top.

March 30, 2021

Progress can be subtle and requires patience. It is so quiet you don't notice when you made it to where you wanted to go. Before you know it, the dark days will be behind you, and the dreams you worked on will be below you. Yes, growth can be exhausting, but rest if you need; don't quit. Trust you are always moving forward, and where you are standing today will be behind you tomorrow. Keep going.

AFFIRM

I am always moving forward.

March 31, 2021

Trust more is happening than what you currently see. Remember, you aren't needed to open the doors you will walkthrough. You aren't needed to clear your paths forward. You aren't needed to build the bridges you will cross. Stop trying to distract yourself by attempting to do it all. Your work is to focus on the mindset that prepares you to receive the blessings of where you are going.

AFFIRM

I am prepared to receive my blessings.

April 1, 2021

This April, I am committed to my happiness. I am pursuing my peace. I am letting in love. I am aligning with abundance. I am grounded in gratitude. I am releasing the old and embracing the new. I am making great choices and improving my life. I am developing the mindset that levels me up to more. I am celebrating my progress. I am welcoming miracles manifesting.

AFFIRM

I am already whole.

April 2, 2021

To get good things, you have to allow good things. You have to open up and permit yourself to become the person that receives abundant blessings. Start with believing you are worthy before you receive it. Speak kindly and compassionately to yourself. Mostly don't forget you are doing the best you can. Today declare, "I am a beautiful, blessed being, and I deserve good things, always."

AFFIRM

I am a beautiful, blessed being, and I deserve good things.

April 3, 2021

The Universe knows what you want. It knows right where you are, and it knows exactly where you need to be. Even though things aren't temporarily going how you want them to go, trust your circumstances have a purpose. Focus on the lesson to be learned, the skill to be developed, or the person you need to become before moving forward. Trust the process.

AFFIRM

I am moving closer to my dreams.

April 4, 2021

Life will always test the limiting beliefs about who you are and what you are worth before it levels you up. Remember, some experiences are designed to break you open and unleash your wholeness. You may not be responsible for hurt in your past or control the change in the present, but you can choose to make your wellbeing a priority. Only you can select the path to your happiness. Decide today to be response-able for your future.

AFFIRM

I am on the right path to my happiness.

April 5, 2021

It is human nature to focus on all the doing and discard the decisions that directed you to your winning. Life isn't about struggles, lost love, or what you lack; it is about how you respond. Moving forward requires mental and emotional evolution. Create your momentum by exercising your ability to make responsible choices. Never allow mistakes to take your confidence or hold you back from moving forward. Remember, you never lose; you learn.

AFFIRM

I am making responsible choices.

April 6, 2021

What you reap is based on your actions, relationship with self, and the attention you place on your emotional health. Plant in faith, not in fear. Consider your heart the seed to your life because what you hold in it will be what grows. You cannot harvest abundance with a mindset of lack. You cannot create love with a heart heavy with resentment. You cannot produce peace sourced from chaos. Yes, miracles manifest from dirt, but healing helps with thriving.

AFFIRM

I am healing and thriving.

April 7, 2021

Stop suffering; start surrendering to the experiences sent to set you free from your burdens. When you choose to hold onto the old and resist the new, you make the transformation more tiring. Yes, the new might be different, but getting through it does not have to be difficult. Everyone goes through changes, but what you create from it becomes your most significant victory. Today instead of allowing the challenge to take your strength, focus on creating solutions.

AFFIRM

I am focused on creating solutions.

April 8, 2021

Pray for the skills to overcome and the ability to find your way through. Pray for the understanding to move beyond what keeps you from producing your prosperity. Pray for the release from the past so you can find your clarity to create your future. Pray for the healing of self-compassion that opens you up to love. Decide that no matter what comes your way, you already have what it takes to win. Remember, the Universe has your back.

AFFIRM

I am already winning.

April 9, 2021

The Universe is always trying to give you something of value by sending you experiences to reveal your true worth. For every test or struggle, there is a better version of you waiting to be accepted. Don't be so focused on what you think you want and miss the real blessing of who you are becoming. A person who understands their power to create can manifest their unlimited potential.

AFFIRM

I am unlimited potential.

April 10, 2021

Many people pray for love, and at the same time, worry about rejection. This doubt closes your heart before you even open it. Your prayers won't be answered if you keep replacing your faith in finding love with the fear of getting hurt. If you have blocks around love, you are not ready for it. Get prepared by understanding your self-love and true self-worth; they will show you how to share and receive the best love available.

AFFIRM

I am worthy of all good things.

April 11, 2021

Breakthroughs come from breakdowns because they enable you to change old habits and outdated mindsets. You asked for more, and life is pushing, pulling, and carrying you there. You won't create your thriving until you push yourself through your healing. You won't find your purpose until you pull yourself to the path that carries you to your destiny. You are always being guided to your all.

AFFIRM

I am Divinely guided and supported.

April 12, 2021

Believing in your possibilities can sometimes feel scary. Doubt will always creep in and try to convince you that you are on the brink of falling or failing. Working on your dreams requires commitment and courage. You have what it takes because you deserve to have all that you desire. Step out with faith, and don't let fear keep you from what you want. Trust you are not about to fall; you are about to fly.

AFFIRM

I am committed to my happiness.

April 13, 2021

What you resist will always find a way to persist. Let go of how you think your life should be and pay attention to where it is showing you to go. You are destined to be more and have more. Growth will continually push you toward your fullest potential. Stop playing small. Go big by taking comfort in knowing that the path will be cleared and what is meant for you will get to you. Let go, align, and flow.

AFFIRM

I am aligning and flowing.

April 14, 2021

No matter how strong you have been in the past, there comes a time when you don't feel like fighting. You are not alone; everyone gets tired occasionally. If you need the strength to move forward, focus on your progress. You have won at so many things in life, don't allow exhaustion to keep you stuck. Learn to rest, reenergize, and remember your why. Never quit on your pursuit of happiness.

AFFIRM

I am resting, reenergizing, and remembering my why.

April 15, 2021

What you believe is what you create. Trust that despite what you currently see, things are working out in your favor. When doubt creeps in, focus on the good showing up for you. When you believe that better is possible, more will manifest. Keep your expectations positive by professing powerful words of prosperity and potential into your life. Good change is flowing to you. Believe you are blessed.

AFFIRM

I am blessed, and more is manifesting for me.

April 16, 2021

You are doing the best you know with what you have learned. Today give yourself patience, love, and compassion. Patience to stick to the path that leads to the prosperity you want. Self-love to know that you deserve what's right, not what's left. Self-compassion as you continue to release what does not serve you while embracing a better you. Trust you have the strength and confidence needed to redirect your life.

AFFIRM

I am strong enough to improve my life.

April 17, 2021

Life is not about perfection; it's about persistence when pursuing your path to what you desire. There will be 'go' days, 'do' days, 'stop' days, 'wait' days, 'rest' days, and 'reset' days. Whatever day is today, keep doing the best you can; that's the only thing that matters. Your journey will continuously change. It's your commitment to your happiness that will keep you moving forward.

AFFIRM

I am committed to my happiness.

April 18, 2021

Forgiveness is not about forgetting; it is about removing the heavy energy that remains from a past you wish was different. You don't have to rebuild a relationship with everyone you have forgiven. But you do have to reestablish a healthy connection with yourself. Don't delay building better by continuing to give room in your heart to bitter. Lighten your burden, forgive yourself and others, and freely create your future.

AFFIRM

I am freely creating my future.

April 19, 2021

Struggle sets in when you highlight your pain and lose sight of your progress. Remember, your past hurt can no longer hold you back when you stay committed to your happiness in the present. Change what you create by celebrating your commitment to your wellbeing. Give yourself credit; you decided to get up today and fight for your right to be happy. Take it one day at a time. Before you know it, you will be through the storm and thriving.

AFFIRM

I am through the storm and thriving.

April 20, 2021

Today say yes to the progress and possibilities that are becoming a natural way of life for you. Say yes to the support that is available and abundant around you. Say yes to the solutions that are being revealed to you. Say yes to the growing opportunities that are showing up for you. Say yes to the love, happiness, and wholeness growing within you. Mostly, and excitedly, say yes to the blessings surrounding you.

AFFIRM

I am saying yes to my blessings.

April 21, 2021

Today is a day of miracles because you are grounding yourself with gratitude. Be thankful for the closed doors that redirected you to new possibilities. Appreciate the cleared paths that made it easy for you to progress to more. Love that you have released the harmful habits and are on the way to your biggest wins. Say thank you for the "no," acknowledge the "yes," and get ready for better than you can imagine. You are being blessed and Divinely protected.

AFFIRM

I am Divinely protected and supported.

April 22, 2021

Take a moment to reflect on your progress. This is not to live in the past but to acknowledge your tremendous growth and strength. You have worked diligently to improve yourself and your situation; that should be celebrated. Be grateful you are not who you used to be, and your abilities helped you flourish. Honor your progress and keep trusting the process. You are becoming what you are creating. Cheers to your success.

AFFIRM

I am attracting what I am creating.

April 23, 2021

Don't get distracted wanting more, and forget to be grateful for what you already have. Overcoming loss and developing gratitude are two of the most challenging lessons in life. Learn to use them and appreciate where you have been as you work on where you want to be. Without struggle, you would not be equipped to find what you need to thrive. No matter where you are on your journey, your attitude of gratitude makes a huge difference. Love your life.

AFFIRM

I am loving my life.

April 24, 2021

Instead of allowing your experiences to challenge your confidence, resist giving up. Today reclaim your power to create better by using what you know. You have been equipped to overcome this exact moment. You already have the strength, abilities, and resources around you required for the win. Decide that no matter what comes your way, you will push past it to the victory line. Miracles happen when you create success from your stumbles. You've got this!

AFFIRM

I am creating my success.

April 25, 2021

Living your best life requires you to work on being your best self. Being your best self is not about resisting what is unfolding but embracing your ability to choose. You control how you respond; that is where your power to thrive originates. Yes, life happens, but how you create from the setback leads to the setup. There will always be obstacles; only you can shape what happens after. You can retreat and stay small or push forward and build your big.

AFFIRM

I am pushing forward and building bigger.

April 26, 2021

Nothing outside of you will make you fulfilled unless you decide to find your joy within. No amount of money, job, or relationship can bring you real gratification unless you cultivate it from your soul. Only you can take charge of creating your love, peace, and prosperity from within. If you don't focus on 'being' the best version of you, nothing you are 'doing' will give you what you want. You must be a 'human-being' before you are a happy 'human-doing.'

AFFIRM

I am a human being.

April 27, 2021

Obstacles appear as blocks, but they are blessings Divinely sent to redirect you to the easiest path to your happiness. Before you get impatient, doubtful, or discouraged, remember you asked for more, and you are being guided there. Delays only slow you down to help you find what you need within to win without. Practicing patience is necessary to prepare you for bigger. Remember, what's yours is yours, and it cannot be denied.

AFFIRM

I am practicing patience while preparing for more.

April 28, 2021

If you are dedicated to your work on your wellbeing, you know your wishes will manifest. Don't give up when what you want does not materialize in the timeframe you expected. Focus on your progress. Despite the stormy weather, do not abandon ship. Hold on and ride it out to your success. You were not brought this far to be deserted. Blessings always manifest right after the moment you feel most defeated. Keep going; you will get what you want soon.

AFFIRM

I am dedicated to my wellbeing.

April 29, 2021

Nothing can delay the victory you have been working towards. Everyone can make the changes they want, but it takes courage to have the faith to wait. Patience is important to the process. Let go of the doubt and keep doing; you already got your answer. Stop questioning the "Yes." This is your confirmation from the Universe that it is done! The moment you release the worry about the when you begin to welcome the win.

AFFIRM

I am welcoming my win.

April 30, 2021

Everything is always working out for you. Tell yourself this every time you feel discouraged or doubtful. All your experiences are necessary to your betterment and are part of a bigger plan pushing you closer to your desires. You must trust that you are not where you are today by chance, but by grace. The faster you learn to see the purpose of all you go through, the more efficiently you create your way through.

AFFIRM

I am creating a way through.

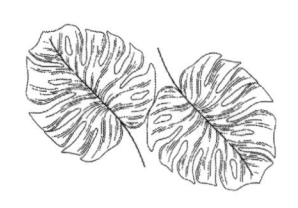

May 1, 2021

This May, I am finding joy through my blessings. I am thankful for what has gone, and I am hopeful for what is yet to come. I am expecting cleared paths, opened doors, and unlimited possibilities to keep thriving. I am celebrating the abundant opportunities for success that are showing up for me.

AFFIRM

I am rejoicing and declaring I have everything I need.

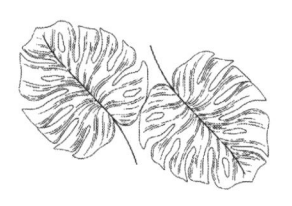

May 2, 2021

As you read this, trust the Universe is sending you everything you need to thrive. What you think you have lost was a lesson in resilience, planting, patience, and harvesting. You must understand how to live without, to treasure living with what you desire. How else will you appreciate the peace, love, and abundance that is coming your way? Experiences in lack teach you the importance of growing your gratitude. Keep going. You've got this.

AFFIRM

I am growing in gratitude.

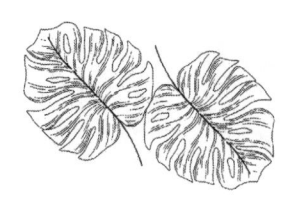

May 3, 2021

You grow what you fertilize. If you keep feeding your fear, you will keep cultivating struggle and resistance. Remember, you are a powerful creator who can transform your life through your responses and choices. Every moment you stay stuck in doubt delays what you want to achieve. Don't let your self-created limits keep you from your unlimited possibilities. Feed your faith, and you will manifest miracles.

AFFIRM

I am feeding my faith.

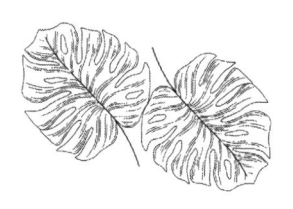

May 4, 2021

You cannot be heard if you don't speak up. You cannot harvest if you don't plant. You cannot heal if you don't address your hurt. You cannot find peace if you don't get still enough to listen for Divine direction. Whatever you are searching for, it is one action away. Stop wishing and start working for it. The Universe wants you to have what you lack. Life won't get better unless you actively create more.

AFFIRM

I am actively creating more.

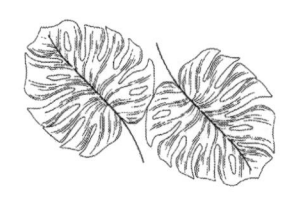

May 5, 2021

Today appreciate where you are standing. Be thankful for the blessings you have and the challenges you never experienced. Sometimes we get discouraged by what we lack and never consider what we were saved from. Stay thankful, focused, and keep pushing forward. You have more miracles manifesting than you acknowledge. Your prayers are being answered. Trust that when you ask, it is Divinely given.

AFFIRM

I am always given what I need to thrive.

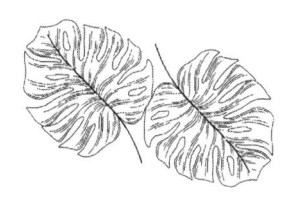

May 6, 2021

Without the struggle, you would never know your real strength. Without the broken heart, you would not have broken free from what was holding you back. Without the lack, you would not have leveled up to more. The times you got knocked down taught you how to find and develop your stance. Today stand proudly in your power. You did that!

AFFIRM

I am standing proudly in my power.

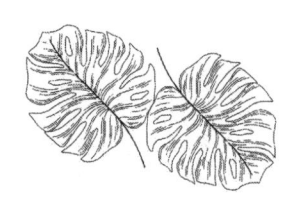

May 7, 2021

Yes, it is hard to make a change after being challenged. Yes, it is tiring to move forward after you have been blocked. Yes, it isn't easy to let go when you want to hold on. But not working on finding the happiness you deserve is leaving you disappointed. Move past wasting time stuck in fear and have faith in the future you deserve. Only you can put effort into your happiness. Start today!

AFFIRM

I am faithful to the future I deserve.

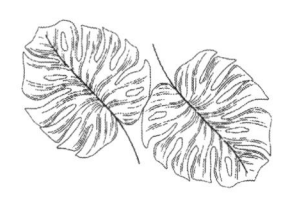

May 8, 2021

Real love is rare; cherish it with gratitude. Anger is destructive; forgive, let go and leave it in the past. Fear is limiting; face it, and move forward to your victory. Worthiness is your birthright, value who you are, and reclaim it at any moment. Memories are precious; cherish them forever in your heart. Life is short; don't forget to live it to the fullest.

AFFIRM

I am living life to the fullest.

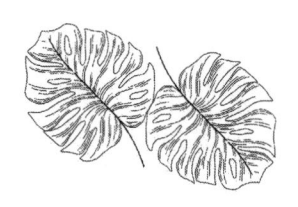

May 9, 2021

When you feel like you are down to nothing, the Universe is silently up to something. If you don't currently see the miracle, stay patient, your magic will manifest. Remember, the fruit is the last thing to appear. Your setback is setting you up for the biggest comeback of your life. Remember, you are always Divinely supported. Trust your harvest is growing.

AFFIRM

I am trusting my harvest will happen soon.

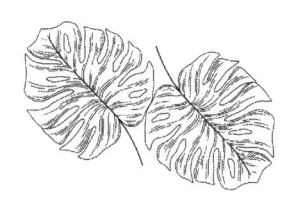

May 10, 2021

The actions you are taking, the inner work you are doing, will be paying off soon. You have what it takes; keep going. Don't doubt your abilities or the timing of your results; have faith it is done, and it will be delivered. Time has no power when you are patient and believe in your purpose. Trust in Divine timing. The answer is, "Yes, your dreams will come true!" Keep believing in yourself and your prayers.

AFFIRM

I am expecting all my dreams to come true.

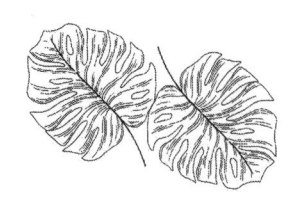

May 11, 2021

Today appreciate where you are standing. Be thankful for the blessings you have and the challenges you never experienced. Sometimes we get discouraged by what we lack and never consider what we were saved from. Stay thankful, focused, and keep pushing forward. You have more miracles manifesting than you know; your prayers are being answered. Trust that when you ask, it is Divinely given.

AFFIRM

I am always given what I need right on time.

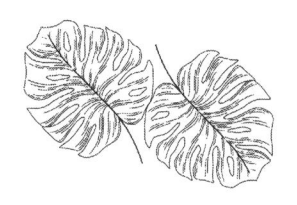

May 12, 2021

Life is always trying to give you what you need, not what you want. When a door closes, be grateful, that was not your way. Obstacles don't mean you were denied; they are signals to look for the opening to more. Don't get so focused on the closed-door you miss your opened door. What is yours can never be denied; it is ready and waiting for you to enter. Embrace where you are; it is where you are supposed to be.

AFFIRM

I am embracing who I am and who I can become.

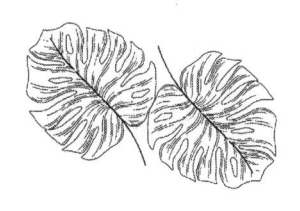

May 13, 2021

Can you afford to delay your happiness? You want to see change manifest in your life, but your fear is freezing you from moving forward. Every moment you stay stuck in doubt delays what you want to achieve. You are a powerful creator with the ability to transform your life. You have everything you need to do this. Don't let the illusion of the impossible keep you from your possible. Choose your happiness.

AFFIRM

I am choosing happiness.

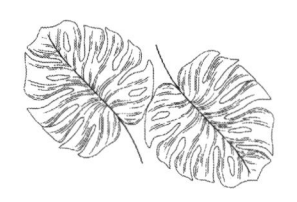

May 14, 2021

There are things in life that come easy, and others requiring you to do a lot of inner work. The area that labors you the most is the one that brings the biggest rewards. Don't get distracted by the lesson and ignore what the final exam is trying to unfold. Education has its levels, and so does life. You must learn better, to live better. You are never tested on what you know; you are always pushed to master what you need to win.

AFFIRM

I am mastering what I need to win.

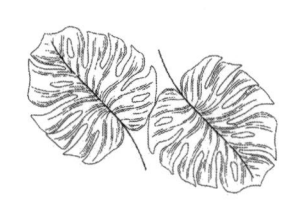

May 15, 2021

Are you focusing on your flaws, or are you exploring your unlimited potential and possibilities? Concentrating on what you don't have will keep you back from going after what you could have. Everyone has something they are trying to overcome, and that is okay. Today look at what you have accomplished and celebrate that. You are doing a great job, my friend.

AFFIRM

I am doing a great job with my happiness.

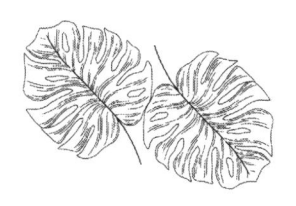

May 16, 2021

Past trauma can lead most to live a life of survival. Releasing, healing, and forgiveness is necessary for stepping forward. Don't let what is behind you prevent you from planting solid roots, planning for your future, and trusting in your happiness. Find your way by shifting from surviving to thriving. Do this by accepting that your experiences do not define you; they only strengthen you. Use what is created within you to create a new you.

AFFIRM

I am releasing with grace and welcoming with gratitude.

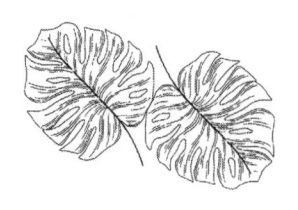

May 17, 2021

No one is coming to save you or bring you happiness. You have to do that for yourself. What keeps you from thriving are the self-imposed limits you created from your pain, not seeing the infinite possibilities of your potential. Reclaim your worth by acknowledging you are capable of being all you desire. Love, abundance, and success are already within you waiting to be unleashed. Confidently be yourself; you are amazing.

AFFIRM

I am confidently saving myself.

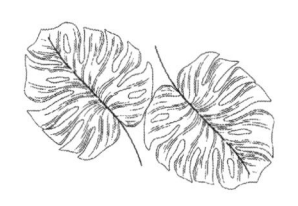

May 18, 2021

If you don't move past what hurts you, it will be challenging to move to what will heal you. Don't be ashamed to work on you; everyone has something they are trying to get over. Healing helps you to bridge the gap between affliction so that you can create affection for yourself. Self-love and forgiveness are necessary for finding the peace you seek. You will find your peace, my friend.

AFFIRM

I am proud of who I am becoming.

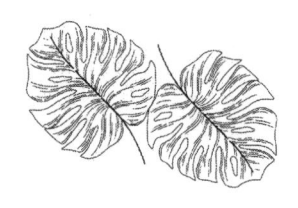

May 19, 2021

Find yourself, and you will always find your way. Let the greatness in you radiate despite what you face. Don't ever doubt your ability to accomplish your dreams. Rejoice in the blessings and Divine miracles coming your way. Purpose attracts possibilities, and gratitude attracts greatness. Today is your day!

AFFIRM

I am expecting a great day today.

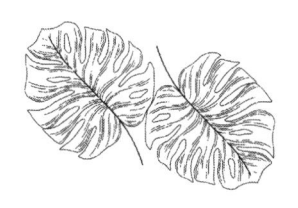

May 20, 2021

Let go of the worry and stress that comes with waiting on the right timing. Focus on the peace of knowing it will happen, rather than the pace it is happening. Life has to go slow at times, so you can prepare for when it starts to go fast. Appreciate the beauty in the pace and give thanks for the peace.

AFFIRM

I am balancing my energy.

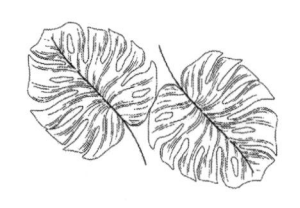

May 21, 2021

You can reap what you sow; therefore, setting the right intention for your life is important. When you make your decisions, create from a place of love, not hurt. Choices made from hurt can create a massive mess. Remember, hurt people hurt people. Before you act, set the right intentions and create from positivity. Miracles will manifest in a life built on purpose.

AFFIRM

I am creating my miracles from a place of love.

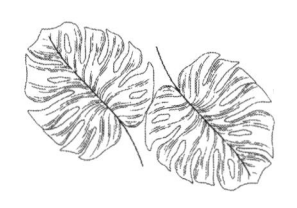

May 22, 2021

Today pray for the grace and dignity to release what you do not need. Ask for the ability to clean and clear without creating another mess. Allow what needs to be eliminated to be put aside with poise. Make room for your plenty by welcoming unlimited prosperity and possibilities.

AFFIRM

I am making room for more.

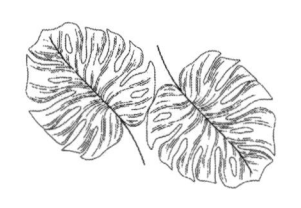

May 23, 2021

Everywhere you have been, prepared you for where you are going. You are born with a purpose, and it is your choice to pursue it. Find yourself, and you will understand your real power. Every chapter of your life is teaching you your capacity to carry and create. There are no mistakes along the way.

AFFIRM

I am always writing a beautiful story for my life.

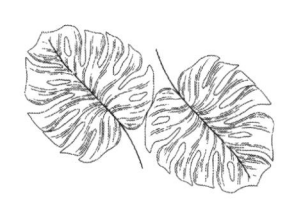

May 24, 2021

Who you are on the inside is important to what you can create on the outside. If you don't feel self-love, love won't find you. If you don't have faith, fear will rule you. If you don't believe you are worthy of all, scarcity will follow you. Focus on who you need to be to live the life you welcome. Most importantly, don't judge yourself while you try. Keep going; you've got this.

AFFIRM

I am doing a great job.

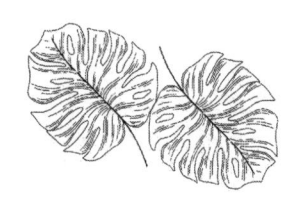

May 25, 2021

Every stumble, step back, or step up works in your favor because they are designed to create a new you. When you think the Universe has left you to fight alone, it will show up with better because it never left your side. At this moment, it is working for you, with you, and ahead of you. Have faith, obstacles are being cleared, and doors are opening. Keep going; the Universe has your back.

AFFIRM

I am stepping into my greatness.

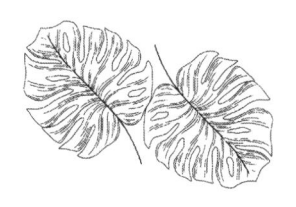

May 26, 2021

Letting go hurts when you focus on holding on. Release by welcoming the lessons and embracing the new opportunities being presented. Doors are often closed to shake things up and redirect you to true happiness. You have what it takes to release what hinders you from your healing. Let go and move forward. Free your hands to create the life you welcome.

AFFIRM

I am embracing new opportunities.

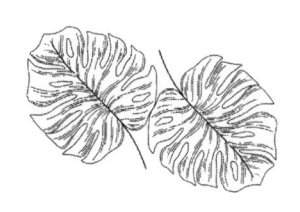

May 27, 2021

You don't know what you possess until who you are is questioned. You don't see what you can endure until the pressure is applied. You don't know what courage you can muster until you have been under fire. The experiences you face were designed to uncover the real you. Don't give up the fight just before the finish. Push forward to your victory.

AFFIRM

I am pushing forward to my victory.

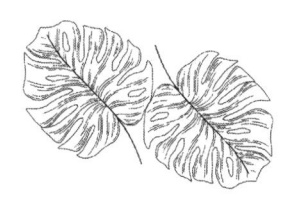

May 28, 2021

When you sit to pray with gratitude, take it a step further by welcoming guidance and solutions. Have a conversation with God today by getting still enough to listen. Prayer is when you ask, and meditation is when you are answered. Move past asking for deliverance and open a channel to receive direction.

AFFIRM

I am receiving clear direction in my life.

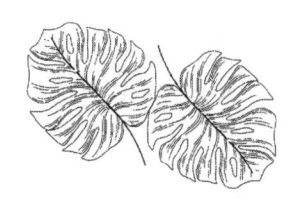

May 29, 2021

Storms always end. No matter how overcast it looks right now, believe in the beautiful blue skies above. Whatever you may be experiencing, focus on the promise, not your planting. Clouds bring the rain that nourishes and creates life. Thank every drop as you welcome your harvest.

AFFIRM

I am welcoming an abundant harvest.

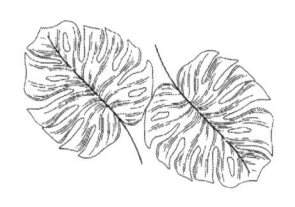

May 30, 2021

Believe that every experience is designed to help you find your true self - the part of you closest to Source. It is not the whisper that says you cannot, but the voice that says you can. It is the part of you that recognizes that your creativity has unlimited potential. Embrace it by understanding you have the power to produce the life you want.

AFFIRM

I am unlimited potential.

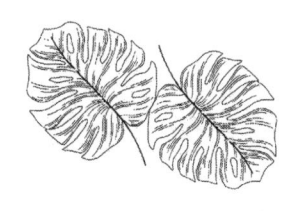

May 31, 2021

Unlock your full potential by concentrating on your possibilities rather than your pain. Everyone has a past where someone has wronged them, or something did not go according to plan. Staying there locks you into victim mode and keeps you away from happiness. Switch to victor mode by accepting you are more than your past and worthy of a great future. You are a powerful creator; start creating.

AFFIRM

I am in victor mode.

June 1, 2021

This June, I am entering a season of more. More connections. More peace. More tolerance. More security. More freedom. More love. More compassion. More joy. More abundance. More spiritual alignment. More blessings. More support. More wellbeing. More upliftment. More grace. More discernment. More laughter. More dancing. More inspiration. More creativity. More me.

AFFIRM

I am more.

June 2, 2021

It's not the times you decide to fight; it's the times you choose to surrender that bring your healing. Forgiving yourself and others doesn't make you weak; it sets you free. Release yourself from carrying the pain of a fight in the past. Stay present and find your peace.

AFFIRM

I am present and finding peace.

June 3, 2021

Stop being vague about what you want to manifest. The Universe cannot fulfill an order it does not understand. Don't ask for love and reject compliments. Don't ask for abundance and waste your gifts. Don't ask for peace, yet keep stirring up the drama. Get clear on what you want to welcome. Specificity and intentionality are key.

AFFIRM

I am clear about what I want to welcome.

June 4, 2021

Hopes and dreams always start as a seed. Remember, seeds take time, nurturing, and love to grow. Getting impatient will not make them flourish any faster. What is for you always shows up at the right time. Keep trusting that your planting is consistently producing, even when you do not see it. Give your seed time to push through the dirt.

AFFIRM

I am consistently producing.

June 5, 2021

The problem isn't the problem; it is your approach to the problem. Focus on the solution. Happiness isn't discovered when you lament on what is going wrong; it is produced when you do more of what's right. You have what it takes to create change. Keep working through and pushing through until your breakthrough.

AFFIRM

I am pushing through to my breakthrough.

June 6, 2021

When life unexpectedly changes, regain control by understanding you have the power to create a new vision. Stop reliving what could have been; focus on the now and what could be. Take the time to heal, focus on what you want, then start creating that. Remember, buildings are built one brick at a time, and your happiness also requires commitment day to day. You've got this.

AFFIRM

I am committed to my happiness.

June 7, 2021

Everything unfolding in your life has a reason and season. Your experiences are only pushing you in the direction of what you prayed for and requested. Struggles set in when you refuse to let go of how you think it should unfold. Release the grip and welcome guidance to get it. What you want is trying to manifest for you; allow it to happen. Stop fighting and flow.

AFFIRM

I am flowing in the right direction.

June 8, 2021

Emotional distraction keeps you stuck. Make your positive feelings a priority, and they will reveal your way forward. Happiness or gratitude will fill you up, energize you, and prepare you to cater to others. Concentrating on the activities that bring you joy is not selfish; it is self-first. When you actively focus on how you want to feel, you will find your mental clarity. Despite what you face, use good emotions to help you thrive, and you will triumph.

AFFIRM

I am creating good emotions.

June 9, 2021

You thrive when you learn to appreciate your lessons, not resist them. Everything you survived prepared you for your purpose and is valuable to your victory. Both trials and triumphs teach you what and who is important to your wellbeing. You may lose people and things along the way, but you always collect what is necessary for your purpose. It is who you become from your experiences that are essential to your story. Trust your path.

AFFIRM

I am trusting my path forward.

June 10, 2021

Many people are great at asking but need to work with how well they receive. Healing and blessings come in many forms, even via trials. Sometimes you have to learn to let go of what holds you back before you level up. The Universe is ALL-ways working to give you what you pray for. Sometimes it does not arrive in the way you expect or the timing you want, but it will show up. Learn to recognize the variations of abundant blessings that surround you. Be open to it all.

AFFIRM

I am open to all good things.

June 11, 2021

When what you do isn't getting you to where you want to go, the Universe will send an experience that pushes you to evolve. Have no fear, have faith that the change is designed to move you to bigger. Stop holding on to what you cannot control and focus on what you can - YOU. Life is transforming you into a better version to pursue the highest vision for your life. The quietest part of you has never forgotten that you are worthy of ALL.

AFFIRM

I am pursuing the highest vision for my life.

June 12, 2021

It is okay to admit when you don't have the answers. Uncertainty occasionally happens. Focus on what you do know and make that work in your favor. Don't let doubt stop you from living or advancing. Before you know it, paths will be cleared, and you will find your way through to the other side. The unknown should never keep you from your happiness. Keep moving forward the best you can. Trust things are working out for you.

AFFIRM

I am trusting things are working out for me.

June 13, 2021

You don't get where you want by remaining who you are. When you let go of the beliefs that limit you, you allow success beyond what you can perceive for yourself. Start by holding yourself accountable for the role you play in the creation of the life you want. You must work on your healing and commit to what makes your soul happy. You have infinite potential. Stop doing things your way; surrender to a new way.

AFFIRM

I am infinite potential.

June 14, 2021

Rejection, resilience, receiving, and redemption are all parts of the cycle of life. Don't get distracted by the lack and miss the magnitude of what is trying to make its way in. Sometimes you don't get what you want, not because you don't deserve it, but because you deserve more. Seasons have reasons, and it is all necessary for your journey. Blessings always follow challenges and changes. Trust in Divine timing.

AFFIRM

I am deserving of more.

June 15, 2021

Forgive who did not know how to love you; they taught you self-love. Forgive who did not know how to treat you as you deserve; they showed you self-care. Forgive who did not believe in your dreams; they pushed you to go forward and self-motivate. Forgive who did not know how to support you; they helped you to self-empower. Forgive and make room in your soul to become the best version of you.

AFFIRM

I am making room in my heart for more.

June 16, 2021

Be grateful that what you thought you wanted never materialized. Trust you were being protected and redirected to more. When you try to create from impatience and chaos, foundations will crumble. What is yours can never be taken away. Slow down and build from a better place by believing your miracles are already done. Sometimes what you wanted was too small for what you are really worth.

AFFIRM

I am being redirected to more.

June 17, 2021

Everything that drowns you teaches you how to swim. Everything that challenges you cultivates your strength. Everything that blocks you pushes you to persevere. Everything that delays you develops your patience. Everything that scares you builds your bravery. Everything that stops you shows you how to flow. Everything that leaves you frees you to level up. Everything that has made you fall empowered you to fly. Fly, my friend, fly.

AFFIRM

I am empowering myself to fly.

June 18, 2021

How you think affects what you create. Today push aside any negative thoughts that cause you to act from worry. If you keep fighting the change unfolding with fear, resistance will keep coming your way. Stay positive and believe the change is working for you, ahead of you, and with you. Life is always trying to give you what you need; sometimes, it is not the way you expected. Release trying to control how your happiness will happen. Just have faith it will.

AFFIRM

I am staying positive and hopeful.

June 19, 2021

When you asked for love or abundance, you probably already got your answer. Blessings never look like the prayers you prayed. The Universe always answers with seeds. Today, take another look at your life and understand the power and potential of what you have been given. The blessing may appear to be small, but with nurturing, it will turn into something big. Seeds are sent to grow you while you grow them.

AFFIRM

I am growing and thriving.

June 20, 2021

Be grateful that life offers second chances, fresh starts, and unlimited opportunities to change course. If you trust the Universe like you claim you do, why do you doubt your manifestations? Stop being impatient by questioning the timing of what you deserve. Your path is already cleared. Your love is already aligned. Your abundance is already accumulated. Your success is already set. Surrender to the process. It is done.

AFFIRM

I am surrendering to the process.

June 21, 2021

You become what you dream of when you embrace who you are. The parts you are ashamed of showed you how strong you are. The parts you want to bury taught you how to push through dirt and grow. The parts that broke you opened allowed you to let more in. The parts that you want to keep in the dark will make you shine. The parts you need to forgive will empower you to forge forward. Every piece of you makes you whole. Love all of you, and you will thrive.

AFFIRM

I am loving all of me.

June 22, 2021

Be receptive to more than you can imagine for yourself by gracefully letting go of what does not serve you. Stay devoted to your happiness, and you will create your miracles. Stay committed to what feeds your soul, and you will achieve your success. Stay patient on your path, and you will develop your perseverance. Stay faithful to the vision of your future, and it will be fruitful. Have confidence your actions are creating your victory. Keep going.

AFFIRM

I am ready for more than I can imagine for myself.

June 23, 2021

Many of you are tired and exhausted from pushing through the dirt. You are ready to give up trying to create change because nothing is happening. Your delay might be because you are going in the wrong direction. Stop pushing backward; start pushing forward. Leave what burdens you behind, release it, and lighten your load. You cannot advance with hands full of hurt. Give the past no power in the present. Let it all go.

AFFIRM

I am pushing forward.

June 24, 2021

Sometimes you get distracted by what you lack and never consider what you were saved from. Today be grateful, not just for what you have but also for what you have never gone through and Divinely protected from. Whatever path you were given, you found your way. Appreciate your ability to overcome and always keep forging forward. Stay thankful, focused, and keep winning. You are more blessed than you know.

AFFIRM

I am blessed.

June 25, 2021

Making that first step to creating happiness can be challenging, but it is necessary. Don't allow fear of the unknown freeze you from moving forward. You owe it to yourself. Just start, stay present, and take it one day at a time, one step at a time. Focus on how you are able, not how you are disabled. Remember, it is a series of continual steps, no matter how strong or shaky, that make up a fulfilling and victorious journey.

AFFIRM

I am taking it one day at a time.

June 26, 2021

Use your words to build your confidence. When you are disbelieving, you are negating your efforts. Whatever you doubt, you cannot manifest. Put aside your fear and feed yourself encouragement, hope, and positivity. Your body is listening to your mind. You deserve to have whatever you are working on. If you planted it, started it, or were guided to it, trust you will finish it and have it.

AFFIRM

I am feeding and fueling my mind with positivity.

June 27, 2021

Things may seem stagnant like they aren't going anywhere, or progress isn't manifesting, but trust the pieces are falling into place. Remember your reasons for starting and keep going on your path. Believe your miracles will happen, and don't give up now. For all you know, you might be one act away from it materializing. Stick to the decisions you have made to pursue your happiness; they will pay off soon.

AFFIRM

I am trusting the pieces are falling into place.

June 28, 2021

Satisfaction and gratitude are powerful emotions that are essential to your thriving. They have healing and magnifying powers that can transform your hopefulness into happiness, joy into ecstasy, peace into harmony, and little into plenty. Focus on the good in your life and use appreciation to amplify your ability to attract more abundance and wellbeing. Whatever you want, you can make it happen.

AFFIRM

I am making my happiness happen.

June 29, 2021

Stop giving doubt the ability to hold you back from having what you want. Look at what you have built thus far and remember your why for starting. Put your energy into the possibilities you are creating for yourself. Remember, it only takes one of those actions to materialize the significant change you want. All your power lies in your right here and right now. Make this moment count. Keep going, and don't stop.

AFFIRM

I am making every moment count.

June 30, 2021

Life is about to change in your favor. Endings are always beginnings, and your potential for new possibilities are unlimited. You are exiting out of one phase and entering into another, and that requires time. Put everything into crafting every detail of what you want; your persistence to your happiness will pay off. It only takes one moment to make everything fall into place, especially when you least expect it. You don't have anything more to do but to trust.

AFFIRM

I am trusting things are changing in my favor.

July 1, 2021

This July, I welcome alignment with the best within me. I will confidently triumph over all that holds me back from pursuing my abundance. I will bravely push past my fears and take inspired action to create my future. I will effortlessly release my need to overthink and concentrate on creating solutions. I will continue to have faith in my ability to find clear, focused thoughts that lead me toward my happiness.

AFFIRM

I am aligning with the fullness of who I am.

July 2, 2021

Put your energy and time into what you are creating, no matter what progress you think you see or don't see. Don't let doubt distract you. Stand behind what you are doing with pride. You are doing the work to put yourself and your happiness first. That is not selfish. You are the source of your creation. If it weren't for you, where you are today would not be possible. Remember, you are a powerful creator; focus on your promise, not the pace.

AFFIRM

I am proud of my progress.

July 3, 2021

Sometimes your trials are significant because they are strengthening your ability to receive big blessings. You will always be sent a challenge that reveals the warrior within you. Trust you will triumph and don't get distracted by the battle. Place your focus on crossing the finish line. When you concentrate on the promise, you understand the fight always has a purpose.

AFFIRM

I am prepared to cross the finish line.

July 4, 2021

When you become disheartened about where you are, find something to be thankful for and keep going. Continue trusting things will change and keep creating that change. Don't lose momentum because you don't currently see results. Keep believing your efforts are producing the outcome you want. Your hope is key to your success. Faith and gratitude will give you the courage to keep going despite what you cannot see.

AFFIRM

I am trusting things will change in my favor soon.

July 5, 2021

There are days designed for you to rest, recoup, and race forward. Resting days are not about inactivity but are necessary to re-energize and refocus. When you get weary, you are being directed to slow before you go. Learn to understand what is needed from each day because every day has a purpose.

AFFIRM

I am learning what I need to gain from every day.

July 6, 2021

Yes, it may seem like you are doing the same things repeatedly, or your efforts feel monotonous, but trust you are making improvements. The paths are clearing, and things are moving right where you need them to be. Use this moment to look at how your life has been enriched and give yourself credit for doing it. You are creating what you want. Remember, progress requires momentum and needs time to pick up the pace. You've got this.

AFFIRM

I am making great improvements in my life.

July 7, 2021

Give yourself more credit for creating. You have gotten up after being knocked down and pushed forward without knowing where you were going. You made breakthroughs from break downs and breakups. Yes, you have more to do, but stop and look at what you have produced thus far. Keep going and believe in the possibilities of your plenty.

AFFIRM

I am believing in the possibilities of my plenty.

July 8, 2021

Today pray with faith and gratitude for the fruitful future that is already prepared for you. Today invite success, cleared paths, healing, and unlimited abundance. Embrace the goodness in your life and work to create more of what you want. Say thank you for your daily provisions and manifested miracles as if they are guaranteed.

AFFIRM

I am thankful for my daily provisions.

July 9, 2021

What is under the surface is more important than what you see up top. If your prayers are delayed, your signals to the Universe may be unclear. You cannot pray for love and don't feel self-love, pray for prosperity yet feel empty, pray for peace, and feel attacked continuously. Get clear on what you want, and don't let hidden whispers overshadow your wishes. What you believe is what you become.

AFFIRM

I am finding my clarity.

July 10, 2021

You have what it takes to pursue your peace after pain. Believe you will grow stronger with every step you take and make the move that pushes you from your comfort zone to your place of courage and power. Your healing is essential to having wholeness and happiness. Life will not change until you change. When your doubt gets loud, quiet it with self-compassion. Trust you already have what it takes to succeed.

AFFIRM

I am pursuing my peace.

July 11, 2021

Be grateful for the opportunities, blessings, cleansing, healing, and progress you have experienced. Be inspired by your growth and your continued focus on what you want to welcome. Be thankful for the transforming mindset that helped you pursue the life you want. As you prepare for your plenty, pray that paths continue to clear, doors swing wide open, and your miracles manifest in abundance.

AFFIRM

I am thankful for my transforming mindset.

July 12, 2021

What's unfolding in your life is necessary for the creation of better. You asked for more, and now you are being prepared and positioned closer to your plenty. Make the transformation easier by releasing your resistance. Endings are necessary to create beginnings, and change is required for evolution and growth. Trust what is coming is more than you can imagine.

AFFIRM

I am trusting big beautiful blessings are on the way to me.

July 13, 2021

Many people get weary when their dreams feel unattainable. This is where most abandon their desires and start over. There is a difference between being tired and giving up. When you are fatigued, rest, don't quit. Take the break to realign, reset, then move forward with clarity, solutions, and strength. Find the test that is causing you to feel exhausted and stop repeating it. Don't start over; master that lesson. Only then can you move closer to your victory line.

AFFIRM

I am moving closer to my victory.

July 14, 2021

Sometimes life has to be broken down before it is rebuilt more magnificent than you can imagine. Destruction is a form of transformation. When something isn't created correctly, it won't be able to handle future expansion. Trust that you are being rebuilt to withstand the weight of the enormous blessings coming your way. Happiness happens when you use your broken pieces to create your masterpieces.

AFFIRM

I am mastering my peace.

July 15, 2021

When you are doubtful, overwhelmed, or stressed, take a moment to pause before you press on. Use this time to pay attention to the limiting beliefs keeping you in a pattern of being stuck. Find your solutions by understanding it is the blockage in your mindset that is preventing you from progressing. Work on receiving clarity and the wisdom to overcome, not for the problem to disappear. You've got this.

AFFIRM

I am receiving clarity and wisdom to overcome.

July 16, 2021

Some people may not want their win the same way you want it for them. There is a difference between saving, sacrificing, and supporting; you decide which one you give. It is not your responsibility to save others, but you can support them by inspiring them. Do what you can, encourage them, offer guidance, but know everyone must save themselves. Stop sacrificing your happiness for others to find theirs.

AFFIRM

I am supportive, and I am supported.

July 17, 2021

Life never takes anything from you without replacing it with something better. Pay attention to your experiences; they are revealing that you should make room for more blessings. If you are being shown that you should walk away from something or someone, run. It is a lesson steering you in the direction of your unlimited possibilities. You are worthy, you are enough, and you are destined for more.

AFFIRM

I am destined for more.

July 18, 2021

Don't let the fear of what could happen; make it that nothing happens. Yes, fear can freeze you from moving forward, but you can overcome it. Believe at this moment, your thoughts are creating an outcome that may never materialize. Get out of your head and stop giving your power to your doubts. Push past the inner distress by focusing on creating a solution. There is always a way out.

AFFIRM

I am focused on creating solutions.

July 19, 2021

Be grateful for your progress while you work on where you want to go. It is possible to believe in your dreams and not be clear about how you will get there. Yes, your reality can be challenging; keep going by trusting and asking for the mental clarity to overcome what holds you back. Don't let the unknown keep you from going after your all. The Universe is always working to remove the obstacles you cannot see.

AFFIRM

I am grateful for my progress.

July 20, 2021

Spiritual growth does not happen when you pray; it occurs when you are transformed through your challenges. In trying times, you develop your patience, inner peace, and persistence with faith. It is the journey, not the destination, where you become who you need to pursue all that you desire. Use your experiences to level up and become the best version of yourself that you can be. When you feel like giving up, remember your fight to be where you are right now.

AFFIRM

I am leveling up and becoming the best version of myself.

July 21, 2021

Releasing, healing, and forgiveness are necessary to step forward to where you want to go. Don't let what is behind you prevent you from planting solid roots, planning for your future, and trusting your happiness. Make the shift from surviving to thriving by accepting that your experiences do not define you; they strengthen and shape you. Use what is created within you to create a new you.

AFFIRM

I am releasing, healing, and thriving.

July 22, 2021

Time always reveals what's yours. Don't let your impatience signal to the Universe that you don't believe in what you deserve. Trust that bigger is coming and get ready for it. Ask yourself what you need to do today to get prepared for your more tomorrow. What's meant for you is flowing to you, and what was never yours is fleeing from you. When it sorts itself out, you will be amazed at how worthy the Universe thinks you are.

AFFIRM

I am worthy, and I am Divinely supported.

July 23, 2021

Everyone has moments where they lack confidence or feel like giving up on pursuing what they deserve. Those are the days that define your persistence. Don't let one day deter you from seeing your better days. You have what it takes to bounce back bigger and brighter. Use the moon as your greatest inspiration that you don't always have to be whole to shine. Show up on your tough days, best days, and every in-between day.

AFFIRM

I am showing up every day for my success.

July 24, 2021

Many people are focused on improving their lives but don't work on who they are or cultivating better daily habits. You are the creator of your experiences; once you understand this, you see that the real work is on yourself. To create your best life, you must develop healthier patterns. No one says you have to be perfect; you just have to work at perfecting who you are. You are the one who determines how you design what you desire.

AFFIRM

I am cultivating better daily habits.

July 25, 2021

Experiences are filled with loss and life, blunders and blessings, darkness and light. You cannot have one without the other. When you expect only triumphs, you don't prepare yourself for the trials. It is hard to understand and believe this, but what you go through shows you where you need to go and who you need to be to get there. Good times are easy, but they are not where you develop the confidence to be fully you.

AFFIRM

I am aligning with the fullness of who I am.

July 26, 2021

Many people battle with believing they aren't good enough because they were told they must be perfect to win. This is wrong; to be human is to be 'flawed,' and to succeed, you must learn flexibility. Perfection is impossible and does not determine value. Stop fighting yourself by putting pressure on yourself to live an impossible life. You are enough, you are deserving, and you can flow and create all you desire; flaws and all.

AFFIRM

I am good enough to receive the best life has to offer.

July 27, 2021

You are getting better; you are flourishing. You made improvements that brought what you work for closer to you. You released the burdens you were never meant to carry. You created the belief in your ability to overcome, and you kept climbing. You recognize that now is your time, and you are showing up and stepping up. Today we applaud and celebrate you for all that you have done to live the life you want. Kudos to you, my friend.

AFFIRM

I am getting better, and I am flourishing.

July 28, 2021

No matter what cards you have been dealt with, trust that you will win no matter what you hold. What you see now does not determine what will manifest in your future. Learn to bet on yourself because you believe in yourself. Sometimes just being in the game and not giving up will bring you the blessing. Be strong, commit to your happiness, and stay the course. What is yours will always find you.

AFFIRM

I am strong, and I am committed to my happiness.

July 29, 2021

The Universe knows every single wish you made and is always working to bring it closer to you. Blessings have a way of manifesting when you release them to Divine timing. When you let go of how, when, and why, what you want will show up bigger than you thought, faster than you can imagine, and more rewarding than you dreamed of. Be patient, allow your dreams to mature into more.

AFFIRM

I am patient as my dreams materialize.

July 30, 2021

Sometimes what holds you back is your idea that 'something' is holding you back. Nothing is in your way but you. Not all your beliefs are real, and they may be what's blocking your success. The faster you correct your thinking, the quicker you get out of your way. Start with changing your focus from 'can't' to constructing. Put all your thoughts into trusting in the unlimited possibilities of your potential. Remember, you are a powerful creator, create.

AFFIRM

I am changing my focus and taking action.

July 31, 2021

Love yourself enough to give yourself everything you ever wanted. Know that while you do the work, you will continue to experience challenges. Don't try to skip the lessons; conquer them, and climb even further. Accept all of your life's trials and triumphs; they are the bricks that build your empire. No moment is ever wasted and will transform you into who you need to reach the summit. The mistakes are where you uncover that you are the magic.

AFFIRM

I am discovering my true magic.

August 1, 2021

This August, I surrender the need to control my life's timing and allow the Universe to bring abundant goodness to me. I am grateful for what I have accomplished, and I gracefully release what doesn't serve me. I am contented with the miracles manifesting, and I focus forward. I am living in the moment with a peace of mind that Source is in control, and all will be well.

AFFIRM

I am at peace.

August 2, 2021

Many people aren't satisfied with what they have, which discourages them from pursuing what they want. How can you get more if you aren't happy with what you already possess? Yes, you may not have all you desire, but your attention to the lack is the same as focusing on the problem and wondering why you can't find a solution. Take another look at where you are and what you have; the answer to creating more is right there. Use where you are to level up to more.

AFFIRM

I am using what I have to level up to more.

August 3, 2021

It is a natural response to see change as challenging. Trust the transformation you are experiencing will not happen overnight, but it will lead to lifelong blessings. Do your part to move it along faster by accepting it and releasing your resistance. Take it one day at a time. Before you know it, you will be delivered to the other side. Remember, nothing strong is built in a day, that also includes you.

AFFIRM

I am releasing my resistance.

August 4, 2021

To thrive is to pursue what makes you prosper. To survive is to give yourself the minimum to live. You have a choice in which you give your attention to. Don't stay stuck surviving because you are waiting for more to manifest. Thrive by making a daily decision to be grateful and stay positively focused on solutions despite the circumstances. Only you can move from surviving to thriving. You deserve to flourish.

AFFIRM

I am focused on my flourishing.

August 5, 2021

If you believe that "when" life gets better, everything will be better, you are setting yourself up for disappointment. The only way to be happy is to feel satisfied with your journey to creating more. You are the same person with the same emotions, no matter where you are or what you have. You are the constant; the journey is the change. Work on how you want to feel and who you are before the results show up at your door. This will make what you desire manifest faster.

AFFIRM

I am satisfied with my journey to creating more.

August 6, 2021

Life is so amazing that it was always on your side when you think it was working against you, guiding you to more than you can imagine for yourself. Experiencing disappointment is where you develop your determination to find happiness. Experiencing a lack is where you appreciate the opportunities to pursue more. Experiencing rejection is where you learn to value who you are. Life will always reveal what you need to thrive before it arrives.

AFFIRM

I am determined to be happy.

August 7, 2021

The person that goes into the storm is never the same soul that steps out. Celebrate that you made it through by leaving the struggle behind. Focus on using the lessons to appreciate the sunlight. When the clouds clear, the sun will shine and bless the next version of you. Staying positive on your journey makes you a powerful creator on your path. You owe it to yourself to go after everything you prayed for in the rain. Go get it.

AFFIRM

I am a powerful creator on my path to more.

August 8, 2021

It is impossible to learn everything at once; this is why life develops your strength a single setback at a time. If you cannot overcome one challenge, you won't manage the abundance of the blessings you prayed for. Happiness is not when everything falls into place. It is about recognizing the miracle of the pieces around you that are already being positioned for your plenty. See that you are already blessed. Have patience; what you want is always coming.

AFFIRM

I am already blessed.

August 9, 2021

Today give yourself patience, love, and compassion. You are doing the best you know with what you have learned. You create what you know. If what you know is not serving you, try embracing something new. You deserve what's right, not what's left. Reconnect and give yourself the power to redirect your life.

AFFIRM

I am reconnecting to my confidence and redirecting my life.

August 10, 2021

Sometimes the burdens you carry are significant because they are designed to strengthen you for big blessings. You will always be sent a challenge that reveals the warrior within you. Triumph by not getting distracted with the battle but by focusing on the victory. When you concentrate on the promise, you understand the fight always has a purpose.

AFFIRM

I am ready for big blessings.

August 11, 2021

Everyone chases what they think is lacking in their lives. You are taught to look on the outside for what you have not discovered on the inside. Stop looking for love and happiness without, because it is already within fighting to come out. You are amazing. Take the time today to go within and discover your greatness.

AFFIRM

I am taking the time to discover my greatness.

August 12, 2021

Finding your purpose begins with looking at the one thing that is unique to you. You overlook it because it is the most natural thing for you to create. Every up, down, yes, and no has taught you something; focus on the message as it is the secret to your fulfillment. The lesson that is taking you the longest to learn unlocks your purpose.

AFFIRM

I am unlocking my full potential.

August 13, 2021

Today say yes to the peace and prosperity that is becoming a natural way of life for you. Say yes to the love that's available and abundant around you. Say yes to the purpose that is being revealed to you. Say yes to the support and the growing opportunities that show up for you. Say yes to the healing and wholeness growing within you. Mostly and triumphantly, say yes to all the blessings making their way to you.

AFFIRM

I am saying yes to peace and prosperity.

August 14, 2021

Do not disregard a blessing that starts as meager. Everyone prays for big things to manifest but don't recognize the power in the 'small.' The talents or abilities you see as insignificant have the potential for bringing you more. Those hard times you overcame, those lessons you learned, they strengthened your abilities within. With time and nurturing, your small will grow into your ALL.

AFFIRM

I am growing my all.

August 15, 2021

Don't doubt your talents; they were not given to be hidden. How else will you be seen if you don't present yourself? Don't wait to be discovered; have faith in your ability to create your opportunities to thrive. Focus on sharing, not perfection, then be patient as the momentum builds. The Universe wants to bless you with unlimited possibilities to prosper. Make room for it by believing in what you were given. Step out, show up, and shine.

AFFIRM

I am stepping out, showing up, and shining at my brightest.

August 16, 2021

Everyone gets exhausted and wants to give up, but just beyond that moment of weariness is your win. There is a difference between giving up and taking a rest. Today, take a minute to regroup, recharge, reset and find what will empower you to push forward. Refuel your mind, body, and spirit before you move forward. Sometimes you must go through neutral before you push it into drive.

AFFIRM

I am allowing myself to rest and reset before I step forward.

August 17, 2021

Obstacles are blessings. They appear as
Obstacles are blessings. They appear as
blocks, but they are Divinely sent to redirect
you to the easiest path to your happiness.
Before you get impatient, doubtful, or
discouraged, remember you asked for more;
you are being guided there. Delays slow you
down because you need to practice patience
while preparing for the bigger. Remember,
what's yours is yours and cannot be denied.

AFFIRM

I am ALL ways being blessed.

August 18, 2021

Be grateful for your blessings while you work on more. The reality of the lack can be challenging at times; keep trusting and asking for the ability to overcome the doubt. It is possible to believe in your dreams yet be hesitant about how you will get there. Don't let that stop you from going after your all. The Universe is always working to remove the obstacles you cannot see.

AFFIRM

I am grateful, and I am being blessed with more.

August 19, 2021

Say goodbye to what wants to go; release it with grace. Say hello to the blessings coming; welcome them with gratitude. Focus on what is present; trust more will come. When you think you were neglected, the Universe will show you it was silently preparing more than you can imagine. Don't lose hope because you cannot see a way, rejoice and expect your miracle. You are always given what you need to thrive.

AFFIRM

I am always given what I need to thrive.

August 20, 2021

The moon is the greatest example that you don't have to be whole every day to shine. Everyone has moments when they lack confidence or feel like giving up. Those are the days that define your persistence. Don't let one day deter you from seeing your better days. You have what it takes to bounce back bigger and brighter. Show up on your tough days, best days, and every in-between day.

AFFIRM

I am showing up for my happiness.

August 21, 2021

Everyone wants something they believe will make them feel good when they get it. They cannot wait for the feeling of success, but that is the cause of impatience. Try feeling successful now and see how easily the victory flows to you. When you feel good before what you want materializes, you will be amazed at how fast the Universe will serve it up. You must feel like a winner before you welcome your win.

AFFIRM

I am a winner, and I know it.

August 22, 2021

You are getting better; you are flourishing. You are making improvements that bring what you work for closer to you. You have released the burdens you were never meant to carry. You have created a belief in your ability to overcome, and you keep climbing. You recognize that now is your time and you are showing up and stepping up. Today we want to applaud you! We celebrate you and all that you have done to live the life you want. Kudos to you my friend.

AFFIRM

I am celebrating my commitment to my happiness.

August 23, 2021

Fights are necessary to reveal the warrior within and strengthen your focus. The art of war says to concentrate on the plan for victory and not get distracted by the battle's difficulty.

When you focus on your promise, you understand the fight has a purpose. Choose strategy over struggle and welcome success.

AFFIRM

I am welcoming big wins.

August 24, 2021

Setups and setbacks are continuous because they are the cycle of life. Learning to embrace the constant change is the lesson that we all take the longest to learn. Have faith in the process because every up, down, back, and forth has a purpose. Believe things are working out for you to learn and get to more of what you want faster. You've got this.

AFFIRM

I am faithful that things are working out in my favor.

August 25, 2021

Do not choose misery over miracles because you are not willing to put in the work. Many are stuck in places they do not want because they refuse to push themselves to higher. Your miracle is one action away. Don't let struggle keep you from making that key step to your success. Don't wish for it; work for it.

AFFIRM

I am working on my win.

August 26, 2021

When you begin to understand what you are worth, your life transforms beyond your self-imposed limits. The belief that you are deserving of ALL allows you to reach for more, welcome more, and go after more. You define how valuable you are to yourself first, and as a result, set the expectation for others. Find your true worth and welcome others to meet you there. You are priceless, start practicing that.

AFFIRM

I am worthy, and I am priceless.

August 27, 2021

When life presents an upheaval, it is only shaking you out of your comfort zone. You are not being penalized for wanting safety; you are being invited to grow. Don't refuse the invitation to better, level up to your bigger. Step out, and never go back. Sometimes the thing you are holding on to is limiting your growth. You may be bigger than where you want to stay.

AFFIRM

I am destined for big beautiful blessings.

August 28, 2021

Mistakes do not mean you are disqualified; consider it temporarily delayed. Remember you never fail, you learn. Use the lesson to strengthen your steps ahead. The beautiful thing about life is that it gives you unlimited chances to pursue happiness. Don't beat yourself up because you stumbled; celebrate that you are still standing. Keep going, my friend!

AFFIRM

I am celebrating that I am still standing and going.

August 29, 2021

Consider patience as a lesson that is designed to strengthen you in the art of receiving. Getting all of your blessings at once can be overwhelming if you are not prepared. The waiting is teaching you the skills needed to carry it all. Trust the timing because the bigger the desires, the more momentum required to create its fullness. It's in the meantime you master the next time.

AFFIRM

I am mastering my moves to more.

August 30, 2021

Life has cycles that teach you to direct your attention toward what you need to thrive in that moment. Each stage is designed to strengthen different aspects of your life. If you skip the lesson, you delay the progress. Focus on what you need to learn in the now and power yourself to move forward. Begin with blessing what blesses you, help who has helped you, and pour into what fills you.

AFFIRM

I am empowering myself to move forward.

August 31, 2021

Pleasant feelings can be easy, but the uncomfortable ones are only pushing you to listen. Pay attention because your soul is trying to communicate with you. You have asked for happiness, love, peace, and abundance; life is trying to guide you to where you need to go. If you are fighting to hold onto something old, imagine the strength you have to create something new. Listen in for the how.

AFFIRM

I am tuning in for guidance.

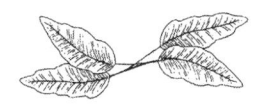

September 1, 2021

This September, I am ready for all new blessings. New partnerships that inspire me to be the best version of me. New opportunities that will lead me to my abundance. New clarity to help me focus on setting the right intentions for my future. New doors will open to better paths and bigger prospects. New chances for me to succeed in my pursuit of what I desire. New peace with my pace and my progress. New mindset that supports my success on my journey.

AFFIRM

I am supported on my journey.

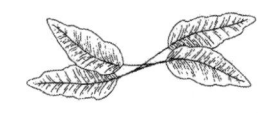

September 2, 2021

Are you seeking to be understood, or are you seeking to be true? Many people confuse the two. When you are looking to be understood, you focus on selling yourself. When you are selling yourself, your focus is on what they are willing to pay, not on what they are actually offering. People who sell miss out on whether the other person is deserving of their worth. When you are focused on being true, your goal is to be yourself. The right person will never need to be sold on your value.

AFFIRM

I am aware of my full worth.

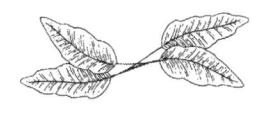

September 3, 2021

If you spend a lot of time worrying about the future, change it by having faith in the wisdom that you aren't supposed to figure it all out at once. It is hard to trust when you don't know how to believe in yourself. Start with working on your ability to BE. BE-ing is the practice of discovering who you are. It is in BE-ing you BE-come the best version of you. Focus on your relationship with yourself instead of the results. You are the creator of those results.

AFFIRM

I am Be-coming the best version of me.

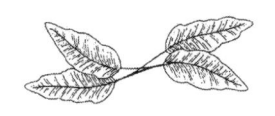

September 4, 2021

When you woke up, did you decide to get ready to thrive or survive? To thrive is to prosper or flourish. To survive is to continue to live or exist. To move from surviving to thriving begins with understanding you have a choice. Thriving is the daily decision to be happy despite the circumstances. Don't stay stuck surviving because you are constantly deferring your happiness to when. Make the decision every day to just be happy.

AFFIRM

I am choosing happiness.

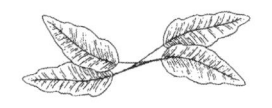

September 5, 2021

Today surrender your need to control because you are Divinely supported. Surrender your fear because you are worthy of what you work for. Surrender your lack because focusing on it is blocking your all. Surrender your stress because it is easier to go with the flow. Surrender your overthinking and embrace the solution. Surrender your heart to healing and welcome the wholeness. Surrender the fight because everything is ALL WAYS working out for you.

AFFIRM

I am surrendering the fight and welcoming the win.

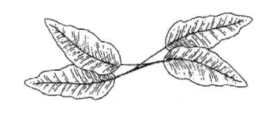

September 6, 2021

The only way to be happy is to feel happy. If you are looking for joy in people, places, and things, it will never show up. If you believe that "when" life gets better, you will feel better, you are in for a tough awakening. A new location, destination, or situation will not change how you feel, only you can. Work on how you want to feel; and the results will show up at your door. You don't have to go anywhere to find what you seek.

AFFIRM

I am blessed with everything that I need.

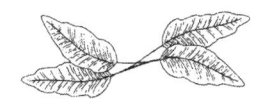

September 7, 2021

Be thankful for every closed door and 'no' you have encountered. These experiences created the strength needed to find the 'yes.' The next time you are stopped with 'no,' say thank you for the rejection and look for the clear direction you are destined to go.

AFFIRM

I am moving in the direction I am destined to go.

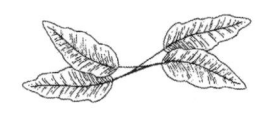

September 8, 2021

You cannot live a happy life when you repeatedly place yourself last. Learn to put yourself first; only then you will be the best for others. No one can effectively lead from behind. "Self-first" is not selfish when it is focused on the habits that support your emotional wellbeing. You cannot expect blessings for things you aren't committed to creating. You thrive when you prioritize what makes you feel good.

AFFIRM

I am prioritizing what makes me feel good.

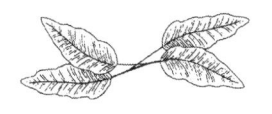

September 9, 2021

Your life is unfolding the way it is for a reason. Don't try to figure out why or how right now; trust you are being guided to what you want. If you desire happiness yet doubt its possibility, you are only moving further away from it. Remember, you create tomorrow by what you believe you deserve today. You can't manifest what you don't think is possible. Trust it is yours first, then it will show up.

AFFIRM

I am trusting then doing.

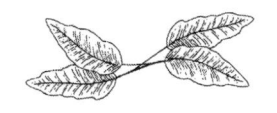

September 10, 2021

When you want love, start with accepting who you are. When you want support, believe in your potential. When you want peace, align with what your soul is saying it needs. When you want to build your faith, push past your fears to what feels right. When you want to move forward, forgive yesterday. When you want abundance, believe you deserve more. Whatever you want is possible; start with practicing its possibility.

AFFIRM

I am believing in my full possibilities.

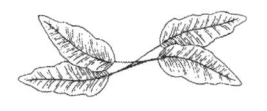

September 11, 2021

Delays are not denials; they are blessings. While you wait, use the opportunity to clarify and fine-tune your desires. Setbacks can help you define what happiness and fulfillment really mean to you. Remember, there must be a problem to solve before you have the blessings of solutions. Life is about sifting and sorting through what you need to thrive. The unfolding is where the biggest miracles happen.

AFFIRM

I am expecting my miracles to manifest soon.

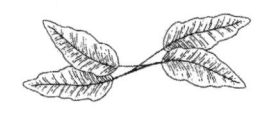

September 12, 2021

When your energy gets off-balanced, it has not accepted your circumstances for what they are. The heart and the head experience conflict because one feels, and the other does not believe. To realign yourself, take a second to listen to both for the truth. Peace will come when you accept a situation for what it is, not what you hoped it would be. Sometimes the heart needs time to align with your head.

AFFIRM

I am accepting life as it is, and I am creating what I desire.

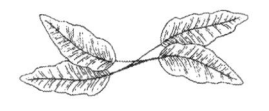

September 13, 2021

You repeat what you don't heal. Don't lose hope when a challenging pattern emerges; focus on the lesson you are missing. Life will keep sending the same struggle to help you overcome self-imposed restrictions. The limits you have developed are based on beliefs about your self-worth, self-love, or self-discipline. Whatever you keep experiencing, compassionately face it, courageously fix it, and confidently move forward to better.

AFFIRM

I am confidently moving forward to better.

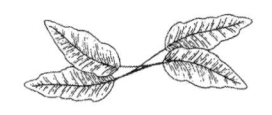

September 14, 2021

Don't take less because you don't know your full worth. When you find yourself going above and beyond because you fear losing affection, take a step back and honestly look at the value you bring. You are beautiful, strong, remarkable, and loving. Believe in your abilities; they have gotten you this far and will continue to take you to unimaginable places.

AFFIRM

I am beautiful, strong, remarkable, and loving.

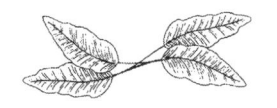

September 15, 2021

You are exactly where you need to be right now. Decide if this moment is filled with gratitude or one spent looking at what you lack. Finding appreciation in a moment builds momentum for lasting happiness. You cannot go back and fix where you have been, but you can choose to focus on moving forward. Thankfulness in the now helps you to build more for your tomorrow.

AFFIRM

I am building my momentum to more with gratitude.

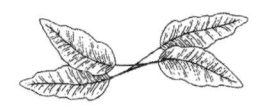

September 16, 2021

You are working very hard to win, but are you putting in the right effort to heal. Healing will bring you the mindset you need to manifest anything. Remember, every experience is designed to advance you emotionally, mentally, and spiritually. Your blessings will only come to a heart and soul that is ready to receive all.

AFFIRM

I am receiving all good things.

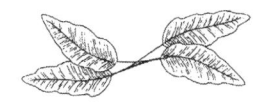

September 17, 2021

If you are struggling, keep fighting; you deserve to move forward. If you have been sacrificing, don't ever give up; you will win. If you feel defeated, remember help is always available; find support. Wherever you are today, believe that life will get better. Keep going, keep showing up, and refuse to leave before your miracle happens.

AFFIRM

I am expecting my miracles to manifest soon.

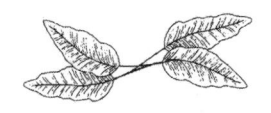

September 18, 2021

Be thankful you are blocked from what you thought you wanted and believe you are being blessed with what you never knew you needed. Trust life is always working for you and with you. It will push you to elevate beyond comfort zones and pull you to levels that force you to release your limits. Stay grateful; you are becoming better for it all.

AFFIRM

I am elevating to more good things.

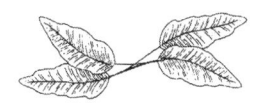

September 19, 2021

"Everything is working out for me," tell yourself that as many times a day as you need. Every twist, turn, up, and down is necessary for the plan to give you what you need to fulfill your purpose. Trust in it all because you are not where you are by chance. The faster you learn to see the purpose of ALL, the more efficiently you create your MORE.

AFFIRM

I am efficiently creating my more

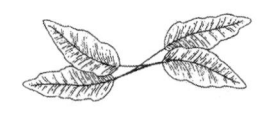

September 20, 2021

Sharing is defined as having something with another. Giving away is defined as providing something to someone you no longer need. Hearts and lives are to be shared with people you love, not given away. Before you give your heart away, consider what it means to share it instead. Before you do, understand you must have a heart worthy of sharing.

AFFIRM

I am sharing my heart, and it is worthy of all good things.

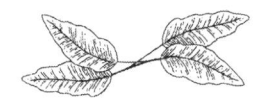

September 21, 2021

When you feel off-balanced or get stuck, the heart and the head are conflicted; your heart has not accepted how your mind sees your situation. One feels, and the other does not believe. To realign yourself, take a second to find truth in both. Peace will come when you accept your reality and pursue good emotions to guide you to solutions. You can create the change you desire.

AFFIRM

I am creating the change I desire.

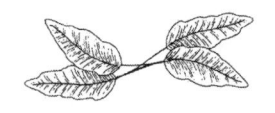

September 22, 2021

Thank everything and everyone that was cleansed from your life. What departed from you was never meant to stay; what remains will make you better. You are not blessed with what you have lost; you are blessed with what you have left. Keep going and using what you have gained to grow. You are deserving of the wins coming your way. Don't forget to thank yourself for not giving up on your happiness.

AFFIRM

I am never giving up on my happiness.

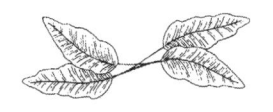

September 23, 2021

Today remember that no matter how many mistakes you have made or how slow your progress might appear, you are still ahead of everyone who has not started. Congratulate yourself for getting up and showing up for yourself. Don't let the delay put you in despair. You will achieve your goals plus more. Keep going. You are a powerful creator, and all your hard work will pay off soon.

AFFIRM

I am celebrating my work on my happiness.

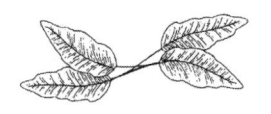

September 24, 2021

Every morning starts with expectations, and every night it ends with experiences earned. No matter how your day unfolds, or what you have or haven't achieved, be grateful for the opportunity to try again. Use yesterday's experiences to make today's expectations your reality. You are never losing; you are being given what you need to succeed. Be thankful for it all as you go after your all.

AFFIRM

I am expecting great things in my life.

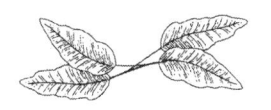

September 25, 2021

Despite what you see happening, trust this storm will end. No matter how overcast it looks right now, believe in the beautiful blue skies just beyond the clouds. Whatever you may be experiencing, focus on the promise, not your planting. Remember, rain cleanses as well as nourishes. Thank every drop as you welcome your harvest. Gardens grow because of the gardener.

AFFIRM

I am welcoming my harvest.

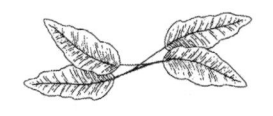

September 26, 2021

Commit yourself to the happiness, healing, and wholeness you want. Yes, you were pushed down, but it is up to you to get back up and push forward. Others can help you, but it is your responsibility to keep standing. Don't stay stuck because you think life is unfair, level up by taking control of your choices. You have what it takes to create the experiences you want, don't let a few shakeups stop your step up to the top.

AFFIRM

I am committed to my healing and wholeness.

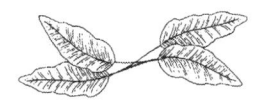

September 27, 2021

You cannot ask for a big harvest yet plant nothing. Yes, the Universe has the power to manifest what you ask for, but you must create the space emotionally, mentally, and spiritually for it to arrive. Decide what you want your life to look like and put effort into welcoming that. Manifestation requires work, not only wishing. Your forest cannot grow and expand if you don't clear the land.

AFFIRM

I am making the emotional, mental, and spiritual space for my blessings to arrive.

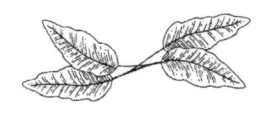

September 28, 2021

Sooner or later, you have to change the mindset that holds you back from believing you deserve more. Sooner or later, you have to release resentment and replace it with resilience. Sooner or later, you have to outgrow the limits that keep you small and go for bigger. Sooner or later, you have to stop wishing and start working on your dreams. Sooner or later, you have to purge the past and start building your future. Pick sooner.

AFFIRM

I am picking sooner.

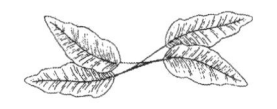

September 29, 2021

Don't allow your old story to keep blocking your new story. Your experiences will keep repeating themselves until you cleanse the effects of your past. Stop rushing to get to the end; you are only missing the lessons that create your happiness. If you don't slow down to face and fix what holds you back today, tomorrow will be the same as yesterday. Only you can make the next chapter better than the last.

AFFIRM

I am creating a new story.

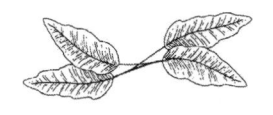

September 30, 2021

You cannot love who you are and dislike the past that shaped you. Who you are today, was created from what you overcame yesterday. Your strength was developed from pushing against your circumstances while pulling yourself forward. Change is never easy and will always stay with you. Remember, the lesson is only your memory; it is not your intelligence. Embrace all of you, to understand more of you.

AFFIRM

I am embracing all of who I am.

October 1, 2021

This October, I am grateful for the opportunities, blessings, and open doors that are already arranged for me. I welcome the ability to stay patient and keep preparing for my prosperity. I am motivated by my progress, and I am committed to creating my victory. I will continue to trust that paths are cleared ahead of me.

AFFIRM

I am expecting miracles to manifest daily.

October 2, 2021

Sometimes what limits us is our capacity to believe that more is available to us. Failure feels finite when we don't think we have more chances to win. Broken hearts feel devastating when we don't believe we will ever find more love. Change feels crippling when we think we are losing when we are only making room for more. The next time you feel defeated, keep going by remembering these words, "There is always more."

AFFIRM

I am trusting that there is always more available to me.

October 3, 2021

Build a faith so strong that you become confident enough not to be doubtful, optimistic enough not to be fearful, and determined enough not to be defeated. Know that what is for you will find you, and your destiny will never be denied. Twists and turns are temporary and necessary to guide you in your purpose.

AFFIRM

I am being guided to my higher purpose.

October 4, 2021

Many people want happiness but aren't even clear what that means to them. Take a moment to find out what you truly want. It is the first step to creating change. Source is waiting for your answer and wants to give you all you desire. If you don't get clear on your intentions, you block yourself from moving forward with anything. Uncertainty is like standing still. Make the time daily to focus on your happiness.

AFFIRM

I am focusing on my happiness daily.

October 5, 2021

Let the word wait work in your favor; use it to master your faith as you keep moving forward. Don't use the delay to doubt; use it to develop the skills to win. Never feel discouraged. Keep working on who you need to be to live the life you want. You are never down to nothing because Source is always up to something. Trust things are lining up for you, and all you need to do is align with it. Your miracles will manifest soon.

AFFIRM

I am ready for my miracles to manifest soon.

October 6, 2021

Stop, sit back, and marvel at the miracles unfolding in your life. Evidence of your progress can appear big or small; either way, recognize your life is transforming for the better. You are always moving forward. If you don't stop to smell the roses, you won't appreciate the garden of abundance growing around you. Today celebrate all that you are creating. Life is good when you see the possibilities.

AFFIRM

I am celebrating my ability to create the life I desire.

October 7, 2021

There is nothing that says you cannot have everything you can imagine. Life sends you what you welcome and confidently believe in. Expect all the love, abundance, peace, and joy you pray for. Ask Source to clear paths, improve conditions, change mindsets, remove limits, provide support, and open more doors. Believing you belong in a place of big blessings is the beginning of the journey.

AFFIRM

I am trusting that I belong in a place of blessings.

October 8, 2021

What will you create today? Will it be happiness, abundance, healing, joy, love, or peace? You are a powerful creator; remember that always. Go out there and create the most out of the life you want, and don't apologize for it. It is your life, not theirs.

AFFIRM

I am creating the best life has to offer.

October 9, 2021

Experiences are where you release limitations. Challenges are where you strengthen your skills. Finding purpose is where you master your talents. Pushing forward is where you develop the determination to fulfill your destiny. Embrace all parts of the process that empowers you to thrive. Whether it's a good day or a challenging day, trust you have what it takes to make it through each phase. Keep going.

AFFIRM

I am releasing my limits.

October 10, 2021

It is not your responsibility to save someone by loving them into healing. It is up to them to heal their own heart. It is your duty to heal your heart then share it with others. Self-improvement begins with self-love and self-awareness. A healed heart recognizes another healed heart and knows real love when it arrives.

AFFIRM

I am a magnet for real love.

October 11, 2021

Don't make decisions when you don't feel self-assured. Choices made from feelings like fear, lack, or loneliness may leave you unhappy. Step back, find what your soul needs. Get clear on the why then the how will unfold. Abundance flows when you understand your worth. Love grows when you appreciate who you are. Support shows up when you believe in who you are destined to be.

AFFIRM

I am making great choices.

October 12, 2021

Continue to work on your healing by finding what fills your heart and balances your soul. Choices made with self-compassion make moving past mistakes more manageable. Don't get stuck on a missed step; keep thanking and trusting in your possibilities. When you practice gratitude, the Universe will give you more to appreciate.

AFFIRM

I am obsessively grateful for my blessings.

October 13, 2021

Faith does not free you from having to fight for what you want. Devotion does not discharge disappointment from others. Hard work does not mean you will never face scarcity or struggle. Being kind does not guarantee you a good life. Experiences are necessary for evolution; it is where you grow. Focus on mastering your cope-ability, and you will triumph through all.

AFFIRM

I am triumphing through it all.

October 14, 2021

Everything you need is already within you, trying to get out. Experiences either strengthen or reveal who you truly are. Struggle happens when you fight the transformation that is trying to unfold in your life. Success occurs when you let go of the resistance and welcome the newly empowered you trying to emerge.

AFFIRM

I am welcoming what empowers me to thrive.

October 15, 2021

It is easy to get discouraged when what you work for isn't materializing fast enough. Don't get distracted focusing on the goal, and miss the greatness gained from the grind. Find what makes you happy while you wait on your miracles to manifest. Amazing things are happening at every step of your journey; appreciate them. Happiness is found in the now.

AFFIRM

I am finding my happiness in the now.

October 16, 2021

At some point, you have to let go of what you think should happen and live in what is truly happening. No one wants to face reality, especially when it's not what you want. But in accepting what is real, you will find the way to move forward. Use what you have and create the life you want.

AFFIRM

I am creating my reality, and it is amazing.

October 17, 2021

Appreciate your ability to create the experiences you want. Be willing to do the work needed to improve what you need to change. You can't just have faith things will work out; you must also have faith in yourself. Show up and meet the Universe halfway by believing you have what it takes to manifest your dreams.

AFFIRM

I am making my dreams my reality.

October 18, 2021

Allow yourself the time you need to adjust to when things don't work out. Show yourself compassion by resting, not quitting. Give yourself room to make mistakes and keep learning. Encourage yourself by celebrating the progress you are making. Keep supporting your dreams by showing up despite the occasional doubt. Never forget to enjoy your wins. You are doing a great job. Keep going.

AFFIRM

I am compassionate with myself.

October 19, 2021

Every day you make choices. Do them from the most empowered state you can be in – love. You won't doubt what you deserve when you believe in who you are. Never wait to be happy. At this moment, you are entirely worthy of everything you desire. You are always writing the story of your life, one decision at a time. Believe in your power of creation.

AFFIRM

I am making great decisions with the life I am creating.

October 20, 2021

You are always attracting the resources you need to complete your vision. Continue to focus on improving your mental, spiritual, and practical application. This is where you will find the inspiration to keep climbing to the top. Trust the Universe is working behind the scenes to move you in the direction of your dreams. You're not far from what you desire.

AFFIRM

I am not far from what I desire.

October 21, 2021

When you haven't developed your trust in yourself or the Universe, you become impatient. When you believe your request will manifest, timing becomes irrelevant. Have faith it will happen and focus on the beauty and grace in the process. Don't block what you are building with doubt; believe in your blessings. It will happen right on time.

AFFIRM

I am building and believing in my blessings.

October 22, 2021

Never lose confidence in your ability to create the story you want to tell. You can either stay stuck in fear or soar in faith. Only you can change the plot twists into your defining moments. Remember, your happiness is your responsibility. No one is coming to save you; however, allow them to support you along the way. Don't give up; keep going. Trust that at this moment, things are lining up and working out for you.

AFFIRM

I am trusting things are lining up for me.

October 23, 2021

Hope is the feeling that things will work out. Faith is a complete trust that things are working out. However, having hope and faith is part of the process. You must add courage to face the facts, patience to find solutions, and discipline to create results. You can have confidence things will work out, but you have to commit to taking inspired effort to work them out. Faith works best with aligned actions.

AFFIRM

I am aligning my faith with my actions.

October 24, 2021

If you think you should be further than you are, it could be because you have not dedicated your whole self to your happiness. Partial commitment does not make a full manifestation. If you don't learn to give all, you won't understand how to receive all. Remember, you get what you give. You already have what you need to succeed. Start today by being all that you want to attract into your life.

AFFIRM

I am fully committed to my happiness.

October 25, 2021

You are on the right path. Trust you are always moving forward, even if you feel stuck or stagnant. Your progress can be improved habits, upgraded mindsets, knowing when to rest and not quit, or the discipline to keep going. Remember, where you are today is further than where you were yesterday. Keep showing up for yourself and your happiness. Don't forget to celebrate along the way.

AFFIRM

I am on the right path to my success.

October 26, 2021

Never be ashamed of the areas in your life that need improvement. Be compassionate with yourself as you learn. Be patient as you pursue the path to happiness. Be gentle as you focus on who you need to become to live the life you desire. Whether it's habits, mindsets, or self-worth that needs work, remember to be kind to yourself as you keep trying. No one is born with all the answers.

AFFIRM

I am working on my wellbeing.

October 27, 2021

Sometimes the reality of your life isn't fair, but it must be faced before you can fix it and move forward. You cannot only rely on faith; you must add belief in your ability to find a way out. Rise up and courageously meet life where it is trying to meet you. You can get through this. Focus on what you can control and allow it to guide you to resolutions. Belief, preparation, and alignment with solutions can bring the results you seek.

AFFIRM

I am believing, preparing, and aligning with the happiness I seek.

October 28, 2021

When you want something, don't contradict it with disbelief. Live with confidence that your victory is already done; express gratitude for the unfolding success in your life. Move past 'asking' for what you need and start 'thanking' for its delivery. Put power into your thoughts and actions and keep creating the change you want in your life. Remember, you are always moving forward.

AFFIRM

I am always moving forward.

October 29, 2021

The Universe is always giving you feedback. When you are not aligned with what your soul needs to thrive, an imbalance of emotions will prevail. Don't discard them; welcome them because they are signaling that something must be changed. Consider negative feelings as a guidance system steering you to happiness. The better you feel, the more you create, and the more you manifest.

AFFIRM

I am aligning with the fullness of who I am.

October 30, 2021

The time between your request and the manifestation should be used for preparing and asking for more. Don't consider it 'waiting' on your dreams to materialize; think of it as an opportunity to keep moving forward. At every moment, you are in motion toward something, even beyond what you requested. Use the time to keep adding more to your dreams. Creation never stops; you shouldn't either.

AFFIRM

I am manifesting more than I can imagine.

October 31, 2021

Always believe that everything is working out for you. When you think that things are falling apart, understand they are miraculously falling into place. Sometimes foundations must break before you can rebuild and become the best version of you. Life will upgrade and transform you for your promise of abundance. Purpose attracts possibilities, and gratitude attracts greatness. Today is your day!

AFFIRM

I am attracting greatness because I am grateful.

November 1, 2021

This November, I am centering myself with Divine grace and gratitude for my blessings. I am faith-full that everything is working out for me. As I release the thoughts that do not serve my happiness, I welcome the pouring of prosperity and wellbeing into my life. My heart and soul are at peace because I trust life is for me. Thank you, Source, for protecting, supporting, providing for, and loving me always.

AFFIRM

I am always loved.

November 2, 2021

When you get close to your victory line, someone or something is always sent to distract you from crossing. Stay focused, and don't let it steer you off course. Today declare, "Nothing will stop my victory, not today!" Keep going.

AFFIRM

I am destined to be victorious.

November 3, 2021

Time cannot be saved for future use, but it can be invested in the future you. What you do today creates your tomorrow. You cannot wish for what you want; you must put in the work to make it materialize. Planted seeds are not immediately fruitful and take time, nurturing, and effort to manifest. You have what it takes, don't let doubt or impatience keep you from planting. You've got this.

AFFIRM

I am investing in my future.

November 4, 2021

Find a reason to course-correct rather than complain. You have plenty to be thankful for; take the time to look. One of your biggest blessings is the opportunity to make a change. Life will reward you with twice as much because you worked the bitter and created your better. Remember, gratitude grounds and allows you to grow into your greatness.

AFFIRM

I am growing in my greatness.

November 5, 2021

Your life will change when you focus on what you have gained, not what you have lost. It is human nature to see what is missing rather than what is manifesting. Life wants you to win. It will pour blessings slowly to teach you how to prepare for your plenty. Learn to manage what you have before you can thrive with what you asked for. You are not where you are by chance; use choice to get where you want to go.

AFFIRM

I am preparing for my plenty.

November 6, 2021

Let go of who you were yesterday, embrace who you are today, and build on who you want to be tomorrow. Do not define your now by your circumstances, but by your unlimited possibilities. You have what it takes to empower yourself and claim your right to build the life you desire. Align with your true self by trusting you always have what you need to succeed. You are Divinely supported.

AFFIRM

I am Divinely supported.

November 7, 2021

Doubt can kill more dreams than failure ever will. Failure teaches, but doubt will prevent you from doing what is needed to create the life you want. Don't let worrying about results rob you of the time required to create change in the now. Everything takes time to manifest and begins with the belief that you deserve it. The Universe is ALL ways working things out in your favor. Make today count.

AFFIRM

I am making every moment count.

November 8, 2021

Say thank you to every door you knocked on that didn't open. Rejoice that it stopped you from getting into places and situations where you did not belong. A closed door is designed to help you discover what you are destined for. What is meant for you will open and welcome you. Trust that more opportunities are always available. Blocked paths can be blessings to beautiful beginnings.

AFFIRM

I am trusting more opportunities are available.

November 9, 2021

When you stop doubting when your prayers will be answered, the Universe will begin to surprise you with new opportunities, fated occurrences, and surprising coincidences. Let go of how you think your blessings should arrive and allow yourself to be amazed by life's generosity. Pay attention to the goodness happening now. Before you know it, all you want will materialize.

AFFIRM

I am being spontaneously blessed.

November 10, 2021

Take a moment to reflect on what you have gone through, not to live in the past, but to honor your progress and keep trusting the process. You have learned and created from your loss. You have become stronger and stuck to the pursuit of your happiness. You have made sure you do not repeat old habits trying to get new results. You have worked diligently to improve yourself and your situation. Today be grateful and celebrate who you are becoming.

AFFIRM

I am celebrating who I am becoming.

November 11, 2021

When you ignore your blessings and focus on the lack, you develop anxiety and stress about what's not going your way. Don't let the deficiency distract you; trust it was sent to guide you to more. How you respond to what you don't want, welcomes what you do want. The Universe is always trying to give you what you prayed for. You are in control of where your attention goes and what cultivates. Stop worrying. Start creating what you are worthy of.

AFFIRM

I am creating what I am worthy of.

November 12, 2021

Progress can be big external validations or small mindset shifts leading to the abundance you want. The most important part of change is who you are becoming; this influences the possibilities you can create. Take a moment to stop and acknowledge the blessings in your life. Truly see the miracles manifesting. If you don't take the time to smell the roses, you won't appreciate the garden you are walking through. Life is good.

AFFIRM

I am acknowledging the blessings in my life.

November 13, 2021

Today let your thoughts focus on alignment with what makes your soul flourish. You are the only one that can recognize the wholeness of your heart. You are the only one that can master the mindset that creates your happiness. You are the only one that can plant the seeds that blossom into abundance. You are the only one that can pursue the life you desire. Everything you need is already within you. Align and thrive.

AFFIRM

I am aligning and thriving.

November 14, 2021

When you doubt what you deserve, what you want does not show up how you expect. Asking from lack will limit what you can create. The Universe is always ready and waiting to give you what you requested. After you prayed for something, you are transformed into who you need to be to receive it. Do your part, be open to more. Release the resistance and meet life where it is trying to meet you. You are worthy of having it all.

AFFIRM

I am worthy of having all.

November 15, 2021

Life will break you down on the outside to develop your strength on the inside. Learning to love yourself during the change will help you thrive. Whether what you want stays or walks away, trust you can let go with ease. Remember, what is yours cannot leave you. Use self-compassion and release the mindset that is holding you back from finding more. Only you can discover what you deserve. Knowing your true worth makes you unstoppable.

AFFIRM

I am unstoppable.

November 16, 2021

When you pray, you are always given something to create what you want. Wherever you think you are in life, make the best of it. Do not disregard what you have; it is essential to the creation of more. Always see the benefit of the small because it creates the potential for all. Focus on your blessings; they are all around you in different stages of manifestation. Plant the seeds you have and nurture them. They are what you need to produce your forest.

AFFIRM

I am planting and producing my forest.

November 17, 2021

Most people wait until they've achieved their goals to be proud of themselves. Find moments to appreciate your progress along the way. You live a fulfilled life when you find your joy throughout your journey. Don't limit yourself by reserving your happiness for the destination. Today applaud what you are doing to change your life. You have worked hard for every single success you experience. Celebrate now, not 'when.'

AFFIRM

I am proud of my progress.

November 18, 2021

Let go of what you think you should have gained and look at what you have achieved. People who attach their happiness to outcomes are never satisfied because they miss the beauty in the unfolding. Relax, things are always working out for you; learn to enjoy the flow. What is meant for you will never miss you, and what is sent to you is intended to teach and create the new you. When you focus on your progress, you inspire yourself to keep going after more.

AFFIRM

I am inspired to keep going for more.

November 19, 2021

Learning to embrace change will make your transition into your life seasons better. Understand the setbacks are only sent to help you define what you want when you step-up. Trust that every up, down, back, and forth has the purpose of getting you clear about defining what your happiness means to you. When you are forced to step back, it is setting you up to make leaps forward. Life is a continuous cycle that encourages your growth. You've got this.

AFFIRM

I am encouraged by my growth.

November 20, 2021

We all experience phases of resilience, rejection, receiving, and redemption. Every season has a reason. Resilience teaches you how to bend without breaking. Rejection teaches you how to reclaim your true worth. Receiving teaches you how to recognize and be grateful for your blessings. Redemption teaches you how to celebrate your triumphs. Whatever stage you are in, know you have what it takes to get through them all. Keep going.

AFFIRM

I am succeeding in all of my seasons.

November 21, 2021

You have to put in the work if you want to win. Don't stay stuck because you lack confidence in your ability to produce your success. Your miracle may be one act of forgiveness away, one deliberate step away, one new habit away, one yes or no away. Your 'work' can be mental or implemental. Only you can decide what you need to develop your dedication and courage to go for the victory. Trust you have what it takes. You can create your happiness.

AFFIRM

I am dedicated to my victory.

November 22, 2021

Today pray for the grace and dignity you need to release what holds you back from finding what makes your heart full, and your soul finds its peace. You have what it takes to move past this moment to happier times. You are enough, and you are doing the best you can. Trust your ability to focus on how to create your more. You are confident and very capable of finding your solutions. Your self-compassion is essential to your thriving.

AFFIRM

I am capable of creating my solutions.

November 23, 2021

When you think you are blocked, trust you are being saved from what you cannot see. What's preventing you from moving forward is encouraging you to stay focused on finding your thriving. You are shaped by every challenge you conquered because you committed to the course. Strong foundations aren't created by chance; they are built when you use your experiences to form your happiness. Be patient with the process.

AFFIRM

I am patient with my process.

November 24, 2021

Don't let the fear of losing affection or recognition keep you from expressing who you are. No matter what, you have to believe that the value you bring is always the same. Conditions shouldn't define the significance of what you have to offer. Never discount your time, love, abilities, or talents because of how others react to it. Believe in your worth always. When you do, the right circumstances will show up to confirm you are priceless.

AFFIRM

I am priceless and worthy of all.

November 25, 2021

Create the fruitful future you want with three principles: vision, intent, and inspired action. Vision because you must know where you are going before the way is revealed to you. Intent because you have to find emotional clarity and belief in your vision before you go. Inspired action because you must first work on who you need to be, then be Divinely guided there. Get clear, stay focused on feeling good, and always prepare to prosper.

AFFIRM

I am prepared to prosper.

November 26, 2021

It takes courage, commitment, and consistency to pursue your peace after pain. It starts with believing you will grow stronger with every step you take, but you must make the first move. Life will not change until you change. When your doubt in your happiness gets loud, quiet it with self-compassion. Trust you already have what it takes to succeed. Don't take your old baggage on your new journey. Healing is essential to your happiness.

AFFIRM

I am trusting I always have what I need.

November 27, 2021

Consider every morning you wake up a new opportunity to start over, stronger, and wiser than before. Don't let past experiences keep you stuck doubting your abilities. Leave yesterday where it is. Appreciate today and begin with optimistic thoughts, new habits, and better beliefs. Reclaim your happiness with thankfulness for the ability to do something different every day. How blessed are you to be given another chance to create what you want?

AFFIRM

I am creating positive thoughts, new habits, and better beliefs.

November 28, 2021

Today, set aside the distraction of your difficulties and focus on your progress, not the pace to win the race. Marvel at how much you have grown. Be amazed by the miracle of your transformation. You walked miles without realizing the importance of the steps you were taking. You succeeded because you took chances with small probabilities of winning. It is in the moments you choose to celebrate that you experience joy on the journey. Keep going; you are crushing it.

AFFIRM

I am amazed at my growth.

November 29, 2021

Trust you are never facing difficulties alone. You are always Divinely supported through the experiences that define your worth and happiness. Everything is working in your favor, even when you do not see it. How else would you get clear on what you want if you don't cleanse what holds you back? At this moment, the Universe is working for you, with you, and ahead of you. Have faith that your doors are already opened; they are waiting on you to walk through.

AFFIRM

I am faithful; my doors are already opened.

November 30, 2021

Honoring your happiness builds your confidence. Figure out what you want before you proceed. Trying to create from uncertainty will only make you doubt your ability to complete what you started. Don't try to run when you need to rest; this will make you question your steps' surety. Take a deep breath, tune in to how you want to feel, and let it guide you forward. If you don't know, don't go. Sometimes being in neutral before you kick into drive is necessary.

AFFIRM

I am honoring my happiness.

December 1, 2021

This December, I align with who I am. I am confident in my ability to overcome what holds me back from abundance. I am progressing with my faith and pushing past my fears. I am concentrating on solutions and releasing my need to overthink. I am attracting the resources I need to help me thrive. I am welcoming clear, focused thoughts that lead me in the direction of my happiness.

AFFIRM

I am moving in the right direction.

December 2, 2021

Whatever you may be experiencing, focus on your blessings, not the blunders. Don't let disappointment keep distracting you from your destiny. Find your confidence by believing that challenges are always conquered and miracles always manifest. You were not Divinely guided this far, to be forgotten. No matter what you face, you have to believe in a better future before you move forward. Stay faith FULL, my friend.

AFFIRM

I am always being blessed with better.

December 3, 2021

Express your gratitude today for your progress and success. Move past asking for more and start thanking for what you already have. Pray with an appreciation for the love, happiness, and abundance that surrounds you. Pray with confidence what you are working on is already yours. Pray with faith you are prepared to receive big blessings at a moment's notice. Stand firm in an attitude of gratitude. You are already abundantly blessed.

AFFIRM

I am making progress, and I am succeeding.

December 4, 2021

The most rewarding relationship you can have begins with self. Take the time to understand what brings you joy, what makes you smile, what sets you apart, what inspires you to create, and magnifies your beauty. Get to know who you are by focusing on how you want to feel and let that fuel your unlimited possibilities. Don't run from yourself; take the time to know yourself. Give your soul what it needs to thrive.

AFFIRM

I am giving my soul what it needs to thrive.

December 5, 2021

Don't discard the fight to survive; it created your passion for thriving. Bless the struggle you endured, it activated your pursuit of success. Thank the constant pushing forward; it uncovered your strength. Forgive the rejection your received; it revealed your true worth. Embrace the desire you developed for more; it ignited your fire to pursue all. You cannot love who you are and dislike what shaped you. Embrace all of you; it created more of you.

AFFIRM

I am pursuing my all.

December 6, 2021

Nature provides the seed with everything it needs to grow. When planted, you do not need to keep focusing on the dirt, only have confidence that it is budding. Trust that the Universe has given you what you need to thrive. Move past the worrying about if, when, and how it will happen; know that you are being prepared to blossom. You are never pushed into a position without the provision to get what's promised. Have faith; you will be fruitful.

AFFIRM

I have faith I will be fruitful.

December 7, 2021

Feeling stuck is a sign that something in your life requires attention. Face it and move forward. If you feel unloved, pay attention to your self-love and self-care routine. If you are distracted by lack, work on your abundance mindset. If you feel lost, find your direction by connecting with your inner wisdom. Whatever is holding you back, conquer it by improving your relationship with it. The change you desire will follow.

AFFIRM

I am improving my relationship with myself.

December 8, 2021

You experience disappointment when you let what you want overshadow what you need. Life is always working to give you what you need. What is meant for you will never miss you, and what is sent to you is intended to teach and create a new you. Let go of what you think you should have gained and look at what you did achieve. Don't let disappointment keep distracting you from your destiny.

AFFIRM

I am focused on my fruitful future.

December 9, 2021

No matter how strong you believe you are, you are still human. No one said life is easy, or there would not be any struggling to stay focused. We all want to be seen, loved, and accepted for who we are. Remain confident in your abilities. Today be kind to yourself and others; we all need compassion.

AFFIRM

I am kind and compassionate with myself.

December 10, 2021

You are valuable, lovable, and unforgettable. Don't let anyone take that belief from your heart. Everyone has it challenging from time to time, but that does not mean happiness is unavailable. Every heart deserves to be loved, and every face deserves a smile. Keep smiling and loving, my friend.

AFFIRM

I am deserving of all good things.

December 11, 2021

Many people believe that when you get what you pray for, you will be happy. Remember, when prayers are answered, you then get more to pray and welcome. Life will always keep you praying despite the abundance of blessings. Stop praying for problems to go away and start thanking for the ability to overcome what comes your way. There will always be a need for prayer.

AFFIRM

I am thanking for my ability to overcome.

December 12, 2021

The change in season is designed to test your resilience. Always creating and reevaluating your dreams is what life is about. Every season has a reason for your progress. Changes and challenges are what you need to learn to walk until it works. Life is like a seed without instructions; you must keep planting and nurturing until it finally blooms.

AFFIRM

I am nurturing my blessings, and they are blossoming.

December 13, 2021

Stop trying to fix other people's problems. Focus on what you need to do to fix your own. Allow life to bless you by focusing on your healing. Many pray for deliverance from hurt but cannot see it already exists because they are distracted by another's healing. Their healing will not improve your life or change your past. Only your healing will bring the happiness you seek. Stop praying for change; get consistent at making change happen in your life.

AFFIRM

I am focused on my happiness.

December 14, 2021

If you are steadfast at your work, your wishes will manifest. Don't quit because answers aren't coming as quickly as you want. Despite the storms, do not abandon ship; take control, and ride it out. Blessings always manifest right after the moment you want to quit. Life is only testing your resilience.

AFFIRM

I am steadfastly working on my miracles to manifest.

December 15, 2021

I am committed to becoming who I need to live the highest vision for my life. I have all that I need and want as life flows to me, and I flow with it. As I work on my purpose, I am Divinely guided, supported, protected, and loved. Thank you, Universe, for always steering me toward the best life has to offer.

AFFIRM

I am Divinely steered toward the best life has to offer.

December 16, 2021

When you have been through a season of struggle and stillness, believe the next natural step to experience is movement. Have faith that what you experience today will change tomorrow if you do the work. Keep moving, climbing, trusting, and welcoming your blessings. Don't give up before the miracle manifests. Keep going.

AFFIRM

I am stepping forward to my blessings.

December 17, 2021

Don't forfeit your blessings because you are afraid to manage your setbacks. When life sends a challenge, don't get stuck, push forward, and take control with your responses. Look at your past achievements for assurance that you have what it takes to step over the struggle and step into success. Believe you are worthy and welcome the prosperity and peace you pray for.

AFFIRM

I am welcoming the peace and prosperity I pray for.

December 18, 2021

See yourself on a mission of guaranteed success and change what you pray for. Understand that what you need most to ensure the win is commitment and the ability to overcome the obstacles in your way. Once you master your mental might, you push through anything. Remember, prayer is needed for the journey, not the destination.

AFFIRM

I am on a mission of guaranteed success.

December 19, 2021

You are only moved into your position of promise when you are ready. Everything you have gone through helps with the principles you need to prosper. You must manage the down before the up, the little before the plenty, and the rejection before the affection. Remember, nothing is going wrong. Stay faith FULL; your prosperity is already prepared.

AFFIRM

I am trusting my prosperity is already prepared.

December 20, 2021

When you put purpose into your day, nothing can hold you back from accomplishing your goals. You begin to understand the reasons for the seasons and refuse to give up on your dreams. Today refocus and express gratitude for your valleys and mountaintops. Before you can earn the right to be thankful up top, you must be thankful down below.

AFFIRM

I am thankful for my blessings.

December 21, 2021

Change is feared when you don't trust your abilities. Believe you can create the happiness you want. Success begins when you understand you are equipped with what you need. Do you think you went through all that struggle and strengthening for nothing? Don't be distracted by what you did not get; focus on the skills you learned and commit to crushing your goals. You've got this.

AFFIRM

I am skilled enough to create the success I desire.

December 22, 2021

Never let doubt win. Combat the feeling by repeating the affirmation: "I am choosing faith over fear." Repeat it as many times as you need to and conquer the doubt with DO. DO believe you are worthy. DO believe you have the power to overcome. Most of all, DO believe you can create the life you want. Your life will transform when you change your doubt into DO.

AFFIRM

I am choosing faith over fear.

December 23, 2021

Stop complaining about what you go through and start 'thanking' for them. Thank every closed door because they directed you to your opened door. Being good does not always mean you get good, but you will learn what is good for you. Push forward and be a victor. Experiences are meant to have you question the progress of your life and push you to your promise.

AFFIRM

I am pushing forward to my victory.

December 24, 2021

Creation requires commitment and won't manifest without work. Yes, taking the first step to making the life you want comes with a little discomfort, but nothing will happen unless you go for it. Don't stay small because you doubt your abilities. Go big, brave, and bold and show the world your capabilities. If you don't bet on yourself, no one else will. Go for it; you can do it!

AFFIRM

I am going for it all.

December 25, 2021

Learn to appreciate your lessons, not resist them. Everything you survived has prepared you for your purpose and is valuable to your happiness. Trials and triumph teach you what is important and who is important. How else would you know who has your back? You may lose people along the way, but never your purpose. Trust in your path. What's in you is always stronger than what's happening around you. Focus.

AFFIRM

I am trusting the path to my plenty.

December 26, 2021

There are things in life that come easy, and there are others that require you to work. Don't get distracted by the fatigue of working and ignore what you already have. There is happiness around you; appreciate it no matter the form of delivery. Being grateful for your existing blessings will welcome more miracles manifesting.

AFFIRM

I am grateful for the miracles manifesting in my life.

December 27, 2021

Life is always directing you to where you need to go to accomplish your purpose. The journey becomes a struggle when you push against the pulls and fight with the flow. Let go of the control you think you need to win and welcome the guidance. Remember, you are always Divinely supported, protected, and loved.

AFFIRM

I am Divinely supported, protected, and loved.

December 28, 2021

Have patience today, my friend. Yes, you want what you are working hard toward to manifest itself. But, if you stop and reflect, you will realize that it has already become your reality. Happiness is not when everything falls into place; it recognizes the miracles of them falling into place. See that you are already blessed.

AFFIRM

I am blessed.

December 29, 2021

With grace and gratitude, allow life to remove what does not serve your happiness. Remember, clearing and creation require time. Today, welcome what makes you whole and helps you heal. Stay patient throughout the transitions. Remember, you never lose; you only learn who you are. That makes you a winner.

AFFIRM

I am learning and winning.

December 30, 2021

Understand the power of your mind and program it for success. Get up, show up, and set the tone for how you want your day to go. Know that you are always in control of your reactions. Don't let the world take that from you. Today be your mastermind.

AFFIRM

I am a master of the mind.

December 31, 2021

The Universe is sending you healing as we speak. What you think you lack is a lesson in planting and patience. You must know how to live without, to understand living with. How else will you appreciate the abundance and the beauty of your harvest? Lack is a lesson on learning the importance of living with gratitude.

AFFIRM

I am whole and worthy.

Cheers to a job well done!

You have completed months of a fantastic journey. We hope the 2021 Commanding Life 365 Days of Inspiration and Affirmations helped you create more of what you desire. Great job on pushing forward, persevering, and making your happiness a priority. Today celebrate your victory and the incredible change you have created in your life from your routine of self-affirming actions. We invite you to check out more of our products. Visit us at:

www.ShopCommandingLife.com

Made in the USA
Middletown, DE
19 March 2021